Greece:
Status of Minorities

October 2012

Contents

LAW LIBRARY OF CONGRESS

GREECE

STATUS OF MINORITIES

Executive Summary

Although the term "minority" has not been universally defined, four critical elements have emerged over the last two decades, mainly from a number of international instruments and case law on minorities: (a) the treatment of minorities within states is a matter of international concern; (b) the existence of minorities is not based on law but is a matter of fact; (c) in addition to the human rights applicable to all individuals, minorities have the right to enjoy their own culture, practice their own religion, and use their own language in community with others of their group; and (d) the right to self-identification. A group may be defined as a minority if it meets certain objective criteria, such as ethnicity, language or religion, and numerical inferiority, as well as the subjective element of self-identification. In recognizing minorities within their borders, states cannot arbitrarily deny their existence, but must base their decision on objective criteria and the subjective element.

At the international and regional levels, a panoply of norms, standards, and principles have been developed by the United Nations, the Council of Europe, the European Union (EU), and the Organization for Security and Co-operation in Europe (OSCE) to protect and safeguard minority rights. Such norms, standards, and principles are binding on Greece legally due to ratification and/or politically, as in the case of OSCE commitments. In particular, under article 27 of the International Covenant on Civil and Political Rights (ICCPR), as interpreted by the Human Rights Committee, the body of experts that monitors implementation of the ICCPR, Greece may be obliged to take positive measures to ensure that minorities enjoy their fundamental human rights, including their culture, language, and religion, and are protected against acts of Greek authorities, be they judicial, administrative, or legislative, and also against acts of other persons.

Greece is a democratic and pluralistic society based on the rule of law and fundamental human rights. It is a largely homogeneous country; according to estimates more than 90% of its population identify themselves as Greek Orthodox. Greece's longstanding and categorical official position is that there is no other minority except the Muslim minority that lives in Western Thrace. Greece also contends that the Muslim minority, which amounts to approximately 100,000 people, is composed of three distinct groups: those of Turkish ethnic origin, the Pomaks, and the Roma.

The origins of the Muslim minority in Western Thrace is the outcome of history and law. Its legal status is governed by (a) the Convention on the Compulsory Exchange of Population signed in Lausanne in January 1923; and (b) the Treaty of Lausanne of July 1923. Both instruments have been signed and ratified by Greece and Turkey. The Convention exempted from the compulsory exchange those Muslim Greek citizens who lived in Western Thrace and the Greek Orthodox of Turkish citizenship who lived in Istanbul and those on the islands of Imbros and Tenedos (Gökçeada and Bozcaada in Turkish). The Treaty of Lausanne establishes the boundaries of modern Turkey and Greece. In addition, the Treaty of Lausanne makes provision for a number of rights to the non-Muslim minorities in Turkey. Greece assumed the obligation to grant the same rights to its Muslim minority with no specific geographic limitation.

The Supreme Court of Greece (Areios Pagos) has held that the Treaty of Lausanne applies to the entire territory of Greece, except the area of the Dodecanese Islands, which falls under the Peace Treaty of Paris of 1947. Nevertheless, the official position of Greece is that the territorial scope of the provisions of the 1923 Lausanne Treaty is limited to the Muslim minority that resides in Western Thrace.

For its part, Greece has fulfilled its basic obligations arising from the Treaty of Lausanne towards its Muslim minority. Muslims who live in Western Thrace are afforded unhindered freedom to enjoy and practice their religion individually or in community with others in numerous mosques. The right to education is also guaranteed and secured to all. Moreover, Greece has taken an affirmative action measure to ensure that a certain percentage of Muslim minority students are enrolled in Greek universities.

Greece is a civil law country with a long civil law tradition and history. There is no consensus in the legal literature or the courts as to whether the Muslim minority has the option to choose between Sharia law and civil jurisdiction. In practice, the Muslim minority is subject to Sharia law, although Sharia law is inconsistent with the principle of equality of the sexes, equality before the law, and international human rights and freedoms. Application of Sharia law to issues of marriage, divorce, guardianship, and inheritance could also be found to violate Greek public order and morals, and is incompatible with EU and Council of Europe rules and standards.

The Lausanne Treaty and Turkey

Article 45 of the Treaty of Lausanne, which according to Greece and Turkey deals with reciprocity, has been contentious from the very beginning. The term "reciprocity" as such does not appear in the language of the Treaty; rather, the word "similarly" is used, which implies parallel obligations rather than making conditional the obligations of each party toward its minorities upon the performance of certain actions by the other party. Consequently, both parties have misconstrued and negatively interpreted article 45, guided by political expediency, and have resorted to the reciprocity principle to justify discriminatory practices against their respective minorities. The volatile period of the 1950s, 1960s, and 1970s in Greece and Turkey's history had an adverse impact on minorities. Reciprocity was often invoked for reasons related to education, religious rights, and religious foundations (vakfs). In contrast to prior law, Greek legislation on vakfs adopted in 2008 contains no reference to the reciprocity clause, indicating that Greece is moving away from it.

The question of reciprocity was raised by Turkey in three cases that reached the European Court of Human Rights (ECHR) in recent years. In 2008, in the case of Apostolidis and Others v. Turkey, *the ECHR stated that the European Convention for the Protection of Human Rights and Fundamental Freedoms (ECHRFF), "contrary to classical international treaties, transcends the frame of simple reciprocity between the contracting parties and creates objective requirements with a collective guarantee that goes beyond the bilateral synallagmatic commitments." This court dictum is significant in itself and has legal implications, because the ECHR clearly denounced reciprocity and sent a message to both parties that state interference with the enjoyment of minority rights will not be accepted by the Court.*

Individuals of Turkish ethnic background argued before the ECHR for the right of self-identification as a "Turkish" minority. Greece has responded to this demand by claiming that the Treaty of Lausanne recognizes only a Muslim minority and not a Turkish one. Consequently, associations wishing to register as "Turkish" are denied registration by Greek courts (including the Supreme Court, which upheld decisions of lower courts) or are ordered to close down on the grounds of public security and public order, as was the case with Tourkiki Enosi Xanthis (the Turkish Union of Xanthi). In three cases—Bekir Ousta, Emin and Others, and Turkish Union of Xanthi—the ECHR found against Greece for infringing the right of association as protected by the European Convention of Human Rights and Fundamental Freedoms. In the aftermath of these cases, and during the period of 2008–2010, thirty-two out of thirty-three applications for registration with the word "minority" have been accepted.

'Macedonian Minority'

Minorities exist as a matter of fact and not of law. This principle was first established by the Permanent Court of International Justice (PCIJ), the predecessor to the International Court of Justice and upheld in subsequent court decisions, including those of the ECHR.

Greece vehemently denies that a distinct ethnic or linguistic minority exists within its borders by the name "Macedonian." However, Greece does recognize an individual's right to self-identification. Recognition of a "Macedonian minority" entails complex political ramifications and Greece has refused to do so, citing public security and public order. The applicants in the case of Sidiropoulos and Others v. Greece, *who established an association called the Home of Macedonian Civilization, instituted legal proceedings before the ECHR arguing for their right to self-identify as a "Macedonian minority" and their right to form associations. The ECHR held that the aims of the association to maintain its culture and traditions "were perfectly clear and legitimate." It also dismissed Greece's arguments and concluded that Greece violated the group's right of association under article 11 of the European Convention on Human Rights. Another case involved Ouranio Toxo (Rainbow), a political party that resorted to the ECHR alleging a violation of the right to association. The ECHR ruled in favor of Ouranio Toxo.*

Roma

While the Roma located in Thrace are granted minority status based on the Treaty of Lausanne of 1923, Roma living in other parts of Greece have been deemed by the Greek government as a "vulnerable group." Greece has instituted a number of public policy programs, including home loans, to assist the Roma in fighting marginalization and social exclusion, and in joining mainstream society. Nevertheless, the European Committee of Social Rights, which is in charge of ensuring implementation of the European Social Charter, found against Greece in 2003 and 2009 for failing to take measures to improve the living conditions of the Roma, especially because of "excessive numbers of Roma living in sub-standard housing conditions," and forced evictions. In the Sampanis *case eleven applicants of Roma origin argued before the ECHR that their children were subject to discrimination and less favorable conditions than other children in school. In 2008, the ECHR court upheld the right of Roma children not to be segregated in schools. The case of* Demir Ibishi and Others v. Greece, *involving sixteen Albanian Roma who were evicted twice, was rejected as inadmissible by the ECHR in April 2012 for failing to exhaust domestic remedies.*

Developments After the Lausanne Treaty Legal Framework

The political and legal landscape has changed dramatically since the signing of the Treaty of Lausanne, one of the two surviving treaties on minorities under the League of Nations system. Greece and Turkey are members of the Council of Europe, and the ECHRFF is part of their domestic legislation. Greece has been a member of the EU since 1981 and is bound by EU treaties, secondary legislation, and the Charter on Fundamental Rights to respect the rights of people belonging to minority groups. For Turkey, accession to the EU requires, inter alia, respect of the law on minorities as formulated in the Copenhagen political criteria of 1993, which was adopted by the European Council.

As stated above, as a state party to the ICCPR, the International Convention on the Elimination of All Forms of Racial Discrimination (CERD), and the Rights of the Child Convention, Greece is required to safeguard certain rights for its minorities. Overarching themes include the right of persons belonging to minorities to practice their own religion, culture, and language.

Moreover, as a participating state in the OSCE, Greece has assumed political commitments under article VII of the Final Act of the Conference on Security and Cooperation in Europe (Helsinki Accords) to protect the rights of minorities within its territory. The Concluding Document of the 1989 Vienna meeting of the OSCE requires protection of the rights of minorities. In addition, the 1990 OSCE Copenhagen document contains political commitments for Greece with regard to minorities. Finally, in the 1990 Charter of Paris for a New Europe, Greece, along with thirty-four other countries, reaffirmed that the ethnic, cultural, linguistic, and religious identity of national minorities "will be protected" and that such persons have the right to express, preserve, and develop that identity in full equality before the law and without any discrimination.

Consequently, while the Treaty of Lausanne of 1923 exclusively regulates the status of the Turkish minority in Western Thrace, the legal documents referenced above could also be relevant and applicable to the Muslim minority. Moreover, Greece has assumed legal and political obligations regarding groups that self-identify as minorities by virtue of the legal instruments referenced above. One could also argue that the Treaty of Lausanne has been supplanted by contemporary legal instruments ratified by Greece that provide specific and extensive minority rights. However, such an argument was dismissed by the Greek Supreme Court, which ruled in Decision No. 4/2005 that the Treaty of Lausanne is a lex specialis *and as such has not been superseded by a newer treaty. Therefore, based on the Supreme Court's decision, Greece remains bound only by the Treaty of Lausanne provisions as far as the Turkish minority is concerned.*

Finally, a number of international and regional human rights bodies under the United Nations and the Council of Europe have issued reports on the situation of minorities in Greece, and have called on Greece to cease its restrictive interpretation of the Treaty of Lausanne and to align its policy with contemporary international and regional human rights treaties.

Juridical Status of Religious Communities

The right to freedom of religion as recognized in the Greek Constitution and the ECHRFF, and as interpreted by the ECHR, is closely linked with the right of association, including the right for religious communities to acquire legal personality. The lack of a possibility to acquire legal personality is in itself a violation of the rights of freedom of religion and association.

In Greece, only the Orthodox Church of Greece, which constitutionally holds the title of the "prevailing religion," the Jews, and the Muslims are legal entities of public law. It appears that other religions or denominations cannot register as such but may register either as associations, foundations, or charitable fund-raising committees pursuant to Greek Civil Code provisions and upon fulfillment of certain criteria, including that of a "known" religion. A lack of juridical status has legal consequences; without it, religious groups cannot represent themselves before the courts and cannot own property.

Pending Legislation on Combating Hatred and Xenophobia

A pending bill on combating hatred and xenophobia seeks to abolish inadequate Greek legislation and harmonize domestic law with EU standards. It is an important piece of legislation designed to cover additional forms of aggravating forms of racism based on religion, color, national or ethnic origin, and sexual orientation committed either verbally, through the press, or through the Internet. The proposed legislation also imposes stiff penalties on violators.

I. Introduction

There is no universally accepted definition of "minorities" under international, European Union (EU), or generally under domestic laws. International human rights law grants minorities the same basic human rights and freedoms enjoyed by others. In addition to the basic principles of nondiscrimination and equality in law and in fact that apply to all, additional legal principles inherent in the notion of a minority have evolved, such as the right to self-identification, that their existence within a state is a matter of fact and not of law that can be ascertained by objective criteria, and that nonrecognition of a minority by a state does not absolve the state of its international obligations.[1]

The question of minority protection is an intricate, politically nuanced, and sensitive issue for states and their minorities. Minority protection embodies human rights aspects and may raise serious political and security concerns in states where minorities exist[2] because of a perceived threat to the sovereignty and security of such states.[3] Throughout history, states have resorted to discriminatory practices against minorities for fear of self-determination and irredentist tendencies. However, in an effort to assuage legitimate concerns and to eliminate any tension between minority protection and safeguarding a state's sovereignty, contemporary human rights instruments, such as the Copenhagen Document of the Organization for Security and Co-

---

[1] FRANCESCO CAPOTORTI, STUDY ON THE RIGHTS OF PERSONS BELONGING TO ETHNIC, RELIGIOUS AND LINGUISTIC MINORITIES 97 (1991); *see also* Document of the Copenhagen Meeting of the Conference on the Human Dimension of the CSCE (Copenhagen Document) para. 37 (June 1990), http://www.osce.org/odihr/elections/14304.

[2] Li-Ann Thio, *The United Nations Working Group on Minorities, in* SYNERGIES IN MINORITY PROTECTION: INTERNATIONAL LAW PERSPECTIVES 50 (Kristin Henrard & Robert Dunbar eds., 2008).

[3] Ronald Meinardus, *Muslims: Turks, Pomaks, and Gypsies, in* MINORITIES IN GREECE: ASPECTS OF A PLURAL SOCIETY 81 (Richard Clogg ed., 2002).

operation in Europe (OSCE) affirm and guarantee that the territorial security and integrity of borders supersede the rights of minorities.[4]

In Greece, as in many other countries, the question of minorities has been deeply entwined with history, politics, and foreign policy considerations.[5] Successive governments have reiterated the official position of Greece, which is that no ethnic or linguistic minorities exist within Greece's borders other than the Muslim minority in Western Thrace.[6] Greece contends that its Muslim minority, which amounts to close to 100,000 persons,[7] comprises three groups: (1) those of Turkish origin, who constitute 50% of the minority population; (2) Pomaks, who speak a Slavic dialect and constitute 35% of the population; and (3) Roma, who represent the remaining 15%.[8]

A common feature of the Muslim minority is religion; otherwise each group has its own distinct origin and cultural background. Greece currently denies the existence of an ethnic Turkish minority in Western Thrace; however, it does recognize that part of the Muslim minority is of Turkish descent (in Greek, *tourkogenis*) but not Turks (*tourkos*), a term that defines the citizens of Turkey.[9] Turkey, as a "kin state,"[10] oversees the interests of the minority in Thrace through the Turkish Consulate General. For its part, Greece also closely monitors the situation of the Greek minority in Turkey through the Ministry of Foreign Affairs. The close ties of the Muslim minority and the Greek minority to their respective kin states are attributed to historical,

---

[4] CAPOTORTI, *supra* note 1, at 98; Copenhagen Document, *supra* note 1, pt. IV (on the rights of minorities). *See also* article 21 of the European Framework Convention for the Protection of National Minorities, C.E.T.S. No. 157 (1995), http://conventions.coe.int/Treaty/en/Treaties/Html/157.htm.

[5] A succinct description of the issue of minorities in Greece and Turkey was formulated in 2010 by a Resolution of the Parliamentary Assembly of the Council of Europe. Council of Europe, Parliamentary Assembly, Resolution 1704 (2010), Freedom of Religion and Other Human Rights of Non-Muslim Minorities in Turkey and for the Muslim Minority in Thrace (Eastern Greece), http://assembly.coe.int/Main.asp?link=/Documents/ AdoptedText/ta10/ERES1704 htm (stating "[t]he Parliamentary Assembly is aware that—heavily influenced by History—the question of the religious minorities in Greece and in Turkey is emotionally very highly charged. It notes that the tenor of bilateral relations between Greece and Turkey during the 20th century largely determined the treatment of their respective minorities.").

[6] *See* App., Comments of the Greek Authorities, *in* Report by Thomas Hammarberg, Commissioner for Human Rights of the Council of Europe, following his visit to Greece on 8–10 December 2008, Issue Reviewed: Human Rights of Minorities (hereinafter the Hammarberg Report), Comm DH(2009)9, http://www.coe.int/t/ commissioner/Activities/countryreports en.asp (click on Greece, then click on DH 2009 (9)).

[7] *See* Information provided by Greece in Report Submitted to the Committee on the Elimination of Racial Discrimination under Article 9 of the International Convention on the Elimination of all Forms of Racial Discrimination (CERD) (Nineteenth Periodic Report) at 8 (Mar. 27, 2008), *available at* http://www.unhcr.org/ refworld/publisher,CERD,,GRC,4aa7b7562,0 html.

[8] *Id.* at 9.

[9] Alexis Alexandris, *Religion or Ethnicity: The Identity Issue of the Minorities in Greece and Turkey*, *in* 12 CROSSING THE AEGEAN: AN APPRAISAL OF THE 1923 COMPULSORY POPULATION EXCHANGE BETWEEN GREECE AND TURKEY 117 (Studies in Forced Migration, Renée Hirschon ed., 2003).

[10] The concept of "kin-state" was discussed by the Venice Commission in a 2001 Report. Venice Commission, Report on the Preferential Treatment of National Minorities by Their Kin-State, adopted Oct. 19–20, 2001, http://www.venice.coe.int/docs/2001/CDL-INF(2001)019-e.asp (in French; click on CDL-INF(2001)019).

cultural, and religious reasons; however, since 1923, considerations based on these reasons have had adverse effects on their status.[11]

The legal status of the Muslim minority is based on the Treaty of Lausanne of 1923,[12] which sets the legal framework for the rights and obligations of Greece toward its Muslim minority and for Turkey toward its non-Muslim minority. Central to the debate on the Treaty of Lausanne is the so-called reciprocity clause, as interpreted and used extensively by Greece and Turkey. Reciprocity has been raised by Greece and Turkey mainly on questions pertaining to religious rights, education, and *vakfs* (religious foundations).

With respect to those who claim to belong to a "Macedonian minority,"[13] Greece often categorically states that it does not recognize that "a distinct ethnic or linguistic minority exists in its territory by the name 'Macedonian.' "[14] Greece also maintains that minority status cannot be granted to other groups because of lack of fulfillment of objective criteria.[15]

Greece's stance toward minorities is periodically reviewed by a number of national and international human rights monitoring bodies. Domestically, the National Commission for Human Rights in its annual report reviews *inter alia* the state of compliance with judgments, mainly those of the European Court of Human Rights (ECHR), and also submits opinions and proposals on pending legislation.[16] The office of the Greek Ombudsman, an independent authority established in 1998, publishes its own annual and special reports.[17]

A 2009 report by Gay McDougall, the United Nations' Independent Expert on Minority Issues, concluded that Greece's interpretation of the term "minorities" was too restrictive to meet current standards and that Greece should retreat from the dispute over whether there is a

---

[11] Alexandris, *supra* note 9, at 126.

[12] Treaty of Peace with Turkey Signed at Lausanne (Lausanne Treaty), July 24, 1923, 18 L.N.T.S. 11 (1924), *reprinted in* 18 AM. J. INT'L L. 4 (Supp. 1924), *available at* http://wwi.lib.byu.edu/index.php/Treaty_of_Lausanne.

[13] The term "Macedonian minority" refers to a small group of people who live in the region of Macedonia in Greece, speak a Slavic dialect, and seek official recognition from Greece as an ethnic or linguistic minority.

[14] Comments of the Greek Government on the Report of the Independent Expert on Minority Issues Following Her Visit to Greece, Gay McDougall, Geneva, Mar. 6, 2009, Annex 3, United Nations General Assembly A/HRC/10/G/5, http://daccess-dds-ny.un.org/doc/UNDOC/GEN/G09/119/60/PDF/G0911960.pdf?OpenElement.

[15] The National Human Rights Commission opines that Greece's "assertion that there is no other minority than the Muslim minority is not borne out of facts." E.U. Network of Independent Experts on Fundamental Rights, Thematic Comment No. 3: The Protection of Minorities in the European Union, Appendix A – The Definition of Minority and Its Status in Domestic Law, at 72, http://ec.europa.eu/justice/fundamental-rights/files/cfr_cdf_them_comments2005_en.pdf.

[16] National Commission for Human Rights Annual Report 2010 at 242 (2010), http://files_nchr.gr/106_2011_eeda_ELL.pdf (in Greek).

[17] The role of the Ombudsman is to examine administrative actions that impinge on the rights and interests of individuals and legal entities, respectively, and to monitor the principle of equality of the sexes. As an equality body, its powers are limited in the absence of authority to impose sanctions or to support individuals who have been discriminated against in court litigation. European Union Agency for Fundamental Rights Annual Report 2008 at 18 (June 2008), http://fra.europa.eu/sites/default/files/fra_uploads/14-ar08p2_en.pdf.

Macedonian or a Turkish minority and focus on protecting the rights of freedom of expression, association, and self-identification.[18] The European Commission against Racism and Intolerance (ECRI) in its 2009 report encouraged Greek authorities to take a positive stance toward the recognition of freedom of expression and association of members of the Macedonian and Turkish communities. Furthermore, Thomas Hammarberg, Commissioner for Human Rights of the Council of Europe, in his 2009 report, *Human Rights of Minorities*,[19] assessed the situation of minorities in Greece and made a number of recommendations. He also expressed his concerns over Greece's refusal to "recognize the existence of any other kind of minority except" the tripartite "Muslim one in Western Thrace" and the restrictive practice of the Greek courts with regard to registering minority associations.[20]

The number of cases brought before the ECHR against Greece has diminished.[21] By December 2011, a chart in the ECHR's Annual Report recorded 1,271 pending cases for Greece, compared to Italy at 13,741, Russia at 40,225, and Turkey at 15,540.[22] In 2009, the ECHR found Greece guilty in sixty-nine cases.[23] By comparison, in 2009 Turkey had the highest number of judgments (356), followed by Russia (219), Romania (168), and Poland (133).[24] In 2010, the ECHR ruled against Greece in one case involving religious freedom and the sworn testimony of witnesses in criminal proceedings.[25] A study that reviewed cases before the ECHR instituted against Greece by the Muslim minority, the Slavo-Macedonians, and the Jehovah's Witnesses, asserts that these groups have resorted to the ECHR not only for legal redress but also because the ECHR is a forum "to express discontent about the position of religious and ethnic minorities on the political and social scene, to publicize their issues and complaints, as well as to pressure the Greek government to change its policies."[26] The study also notes that the judgments

---

[18] U.N. Human Rights Council, *Report of the Independent Expert on Minority Issues, Gay McDougall: Addendum: Mission to Greece (8–16 Sept. 2008)* ¶ 81, U.N. Doc. A/HRC/10/11/Add.3 (Feb. 18, 2009), http://www.unhcr.org/refworld/country,,,MISSION,GRC,,49b7b2e52,0.html.

[19] Hammarberg Report, *supra* note 6, ch. VI (Conclusions and Recommendations).

[20] *Id.* paras. 40, 54, 56.

[21] İbrahim Özden Kaboğlu & Stylianos-Ioannis G. Koutnatzis, *The Reception Process in Greece and Turkey*, *in* A EUROPE OF RIGHTS 451, 473 (Helen Keller & Alec Stone Sweet eds., 2008). The authors note that the number of judgments rendered against Greece reached its peak in 1994 at close to 300. In 2000 the number exceeded 200, in 2003 it reached 400, in 2005 there were some 101 violations, and the number was reduced to about 53 in 2006. *Id.*

[22] EUROPEAN COURT OF HUMAN RIGHTS, ANNUAL REPORT 2011 at 152 (Mar. 2012), http://www.echr.coe.int/NR/rdonlyres/77FF4249-96E5-4D1F-BE71-42867A469225/0/2011_Rapport_Annuel_EN.pdf.

[23] EUROPEAN COURT OF HUMAN RIGHTS, ANNUAL REPORT 2009 at 144 (May 2010), http://www.echr.coe.int/NR/rdonlyres/C25277F5-BCAE-4401-BC9B-F58D015E4D54/0/2009_Annual_Report_Final.pdf.

[24] *Id.* at 12.

[25] Case of Dimitras and Others v. Greece, App. Nos. 34207/08 and 6365/09, Eur. Ct. H.R., http://hudoc.echr.coe.int/sites/eng/pages/search.aspx?i=001-107277 (in French).

[26] Dia Anagnostou & Evangelia Psychoyiotopoulou, Supranational Rights Litigation, Implementation and the Domestic Impact of Strasbourg Court Jurisprudence: A Case Study of Greece, 6 ELIAMEP (Report for the JURISTRAS Project), http://www.juristras.eliamep.gr/wp-content/uploads/2008/09/casestudygreece.pdf (last visited Sept. 28, 2012). The national courts play a decisive role in the implementation of ECHR judgments. The study cites other existing implementing structures in Greece that are in charge of implementing ECHR decisions: (a) The Permanent National Representative of Greece in Strasbourg who is a diplomat of the Ministry of Foreign Affairs and

of the ECHR are often based on erroneous interpretation and application of domestic legislation rather than the laws themselves;[27] and that Greece's firm policy is not to recognize the right of association of the Slavo-Macedonians and the Muslim minority to register as Turkish.[28]

Against this background, this report examines and analyzes Greece's obligations toward minorities arising from nationally and internationally binding legal instruments signed and ratified by Greece, starting with the Treaty of Lausanne, post-Lausanne agreements, and case law, primarily that of the ECHR.

A review of the treatment of the Muslim minority in Greece raises the preliminary and much broader question of the definition of "minorities" and the constitutive elements of such definition. In this context, the report explores whether other groups may fall within the scope of the definition of minority on the basis of religious, ethnic, or linguistic characteristics. A brief portion of this report reviews the judgments of the ECHR pertaining to the rights of self-identification and association of the group that calls itself the "Macedonian minority."

The principal objective of this report is to analyze the continuing validity of the use of the reciprocity clause, as allegedly contained in the Treaty, and its interpretation and application by Greece in light of international obligations undertaken through the signing and ratification of international human rights instruments subsequent to the Treaty and recent ECHR judgments relating to reciprocity. Since 1923, both parties have raised the reciprocity clause intermittently, mainly in the areas of education and the *vakfs*.

The situation of the Greek Roma who live outside the Western Thrace region and thus are not considered part of the Muslim minority deserves its own section, because these people constitute a marginalized segment of the Greek population. In legislation and policy measures, they are considered a "vulnerable group" and Greece has taken a number of positive measures to assist their integration into civil society. This report highlights the status of Roma in the fields of education and housing, and reviews applicable legal standards and case law.

The final part of this report examines the question of religious freedom in general, the relationship between the Greek Orthodox Church and the Greek state, restrictions imposed on the opening and operation of places of worship, and the legal status of other religions and denominations.

This report is based on primary sources—that is, the international legal instruments applicable to minorities, domestic law, domestic court decisions, and ECHR case law. The legal

---

in direct contact with the Committee of Ministers on measures to be taken regarding implementation of judgments; (b) the Legal Council of State (LCS); and (c) the competent ministries, especially the Ministry of Justice, because most of the cases involve judicial proceedings and length of time. The fact that the LCS represents Greece before the Court and at the same time implements ECHR judgments raises conflict of interest issues. The authors identify the limitations of the LCS role, given that it does not follow through and does not oversee the implementation process. In recognition of its inability to provide effective implementation, the LCS has suggested the formation of a joint ministerial committee designed to deal with full implementation of ECHR judgments. Id. at 12.

[27] *Id.* at 3.

[28] *Id.* at 23.

literature and reports of authoritative human rights monitoring bodies have also been reviewed and referenced where applicable. Because minorities exist as a matter of historical fact and not of law, as held by the Permanent Court of International Justice (PCIJ), the predecessor to the International Court of Justice,[29] and reaffirmed by the ECHR,[30] a brief reference to historical events is made only when it is essential and to clarify and frame the minority question within its historical and social context in Greece.

II. General Domestic Framework with Respect to Minorities

A. Background

Demographically, Greece is a largely homogeneous country; more than 90% of Greek citizens view themselves as ethnic Greeks, having a common language and a common religion—that of the Eastern Orthodox Church of Christ.[31] This homogeneity is attributed to two population exchanges[32] following several wars and a domestic policy whose objective was to create a nation-state[33] and assimilate all non-ethnic Greek citizens into the overwhelmingly Greek Orthodox society. The Constitution of 1975, as amended, provides that Greeks living in other countries also fall within its ambit and are under the care of the Greek state, which undertakes to maintain close ties with such persons and to promote the educational and professional advancement of emigrant Greeks.[34]

The Constitution grants to everyone within the Greek territory the right to life, honor, and freedom without discrimination on the basis of ethnicity, race, language, or religious or political convictions.[35] The principle of the equality of Greek citizens is also guaranteed.[36]

---

[29] Permanent Court of International Justice (PCIJ) Interpretation of the Convention Between Greece and Bulgaria Respecting Reciprocal Emigration, Advisory Op., July 31, 1930, Series B, No. 17.33.

[30] Case of Sidiropoulos and Others v. Greece at 41, App. No. 57/1997/841/1047, Eur. Ct. H.R. (July 10, 1998), http://hudoc.echr.coe.int/sites/eng/pages/search.aspx?i=001-58205.

[31] *See* Christos L. Rozakis, *The International Protection of Minorities in Greece, in* GREECE IN A CHANGING EUROPE 97 (Featherstone and Ifantis eds., 1996). Information on Greece contained in the US State Department's *International Religious Freedom Report 2011* provides a higher estimate. According to the Report, close to 98% of the population identifies itself as Greek Orthodox. U.S. DEP'T OF STATE, INTERNATIONAL RELIGIOUS FREEDOM REPORT 2011: GREECE, http://www.state.gov/j/drl/rls/irf/religiousfreedom/index htm#wrapper.

[32] During the tumultuous periods of 1912 and 1923, Greece's territory was reconfigured through two population exchanges—the 1919 "voluntary" exchange of population with Bulgaria and the 1923 mandatory exchange of population between Greece and Turkey. Ioannis N. Grigoriadis, *On the Europeanization of Minority Rights Protection: Comparing the Cases of Greece and Turkey*, 13(1) MEDITERRANEAN POLITICS 24 (2008).

[33] Some have argued that the notion of a nation-state is outdated in the contemporary world and may trigger discriminatory practices. *See* Gudmundur Alfredsson, *Minority Rights: An Overview, in* XXXV THESAURUS ACROASIUM: MULTICULTURALISM AND INTERNATIONAL LAW 291 (Kalliopi Koufa ed., 2007).

[34] Greek Constitution of 1975, *as amended through* May 27, 2008, art. 108, para. 1, *available at* http://www.hellenicparliament.gr/UserFiles/f3c70a23-7696-49db-9148-f24dce6a27c8/001-156%20aggliko.pdf.

[35] *Id.* art. 5, para. 2.

[36] *Id.* art. 4, para.1 (stating that all Greek citizens are equal before the law).

The notion of a national and a religious consciousness has been deeply ingrained in the Greek Constitution, governmental policy measures, and court decisions. Article 16 of the Greek Constitution pronounces that one of the objectives of education is the development of the notion of national and religious (presumably Greek Orthodox) consciousness. Governmental policies have dictated mandatory teaching of religion[37] in school,[38] as well the inscription of one's religion on his or her personal identity card. This discriminatory measure was abolished in 2000 in the aftermath of protests by Catholics and Jews,[39] who had argued that it violated their freedom of religion. The distinction between *omogenis*, that is, a foreign citizen of Greek descent, and *allogenis*, a non-ethnic Greek, which has been enforced since at least 1955 when the citizenship law was codified, resulted in discriminatory practices and specifically the collective denaturalization of members of the Muslim minority. In 1981, the Council of State (Supreme Administrative Court) defined as *allogenis* a person who is born of non-ethnic Greek parents and has demonstrated a lack of Greek national conscience, not having been assimilated to the Greek

---

[37] International Covenant on Civil and Political Rights (ICCPR) art. 18, para. 3, Dec. 16, 1966, 999 U.N.T.S. 171, http://www.unhcr.org/refworld/docid/3ae6b3aa0.html, acceded by Greece May 5, 1997, Law No. 2462/1997, EPHEMERIS TES KYVERNESEOS TES HELLENIKES DEMOKRATIAS [E.K.E.D.] [GAZETTE OF THE HELLENIC REPUBLIC] (1997), Part A, No. 25, http://www.et.gr/index.php?option=com_wrapper&view= wrapper&Itemid=108&lang=el (click on number and year of law) (guarantees the freedom of parents to ensure the religious and moral education of their children in conformity with their own convictions). The Human Rights Committee of the ICCPR has further clarified that public education that includes instruction in a particular religion in public schools is incompatible with article 18.4 unless the state provides for alternatives to accommodate the wishes of parents and guardians. Human Rights Committee, *General Comment No. 22, The Right to Freedom of Thought, Conscience and Religion (Art. 18)*, para. 6 (July 30, 1993), http://www.unhchr.ch/tbs/doc.nsf/ (Symbol)/9a30112c27d1167cc12563ed004d8f15?Opendocument. *See also* OSCE/ODIHR, *Guidelines for Review of Legislation Pertaining to Religion or Belief* (hereinafter OSCE/ODIHR Guidelines)39 (2004), http://www.osce.org/odihr/13993. It appears that Greece is in line with these international standards.

[38] In 1995, the Council of State held that students may abstain from religious instruction in school only if the students (or their parents, in the case of minors) make a statement that they belong to a different religion/denomination. Based on a 1995 circular, students could select one of three options: atheist, different denomination, or different religion, which necessitated partial disclosure of one's religious beliefs. The 2008 case of Alexandridis v. Greece prompted a change in this regard. In this case, a lawyer had to declare that he was an atheist, and the ECHR held that the obligation to answer negatively about one's religious convictions as a condition to exercise a right was illegal. A 2008 circular from the Minister of Education stated that students, regardless of religious convictions, have the right to abstain from religious teaching, as long as they provide a statement that they wish to abstain because of their conscience. Alexandridis v. Greece, App. No. 19516/06, Eur. Ct. H.R. (Feb. 21, 2008); *see also* Press Release, Greek Ombudsman, Release of Students from Religious Instruction (Nov. 17, 2008), *available at* http://www.minedu.gov.gr/ (in Greek).

[39] The inscription of one's name on an identity card in Greece was used by the Nazis to facilitate the identification of Jews. It was again used later, especially during military rule, to identify those who did not fit within the Greek-Orthodox ideal of being a Greek citizen. Following an opinion of the National Commission of Human Rights, in 2000, a decision of the Minister of Public Order determined the data to be used on the identity card, without mention of religion. Joint Decision of Ministries of Finance and Public Order No. 8200/0-441210, July 17, 2000, E.K.E.D. 2000, B:879, http://www.et.gr/index.php?option=com_wrapper&view=wrapper& Itemid=104&lang=el. For more information, *see* CENTER FOR DOCUMENTATION AND INFORMATION ON MINORITIES IN EUROPE-SOUTHEAST EUROPE (CEDIME-CE), CATHOLICS OF GREECE 59 (2002). The 2000 joint ministerial decision drew the Orthodox Church's wrath and strong criticism. Recently, a new identity card was proposed that meets current standards on personal data protection. The Church has voiced its concern again to ensure that no bar code is inserted in the personal card that contains the number 666, traditionally believed to represent the Antichrist. Apostolos Papapostolou, *Greek Church Demands No Mention of 666 in New I.D. Cards*, GREEK REPORTER (Nov. 20, 2010), http://greece.greekreporter.com/2010/11/18/greek-church-demands-no-mention-of-666-on-new-i-d-cards/.

nation, which is composed of all those who are tied together by common historical traditions, aspirations, and ideals.[40]

Based on article 19 of the Greek Citizenship Code, Greek authorities denaturalized Greek citizens of non-Greek descent who left Greece allegedly with no intention of returning. This practice persisted from 1955 through 1998. The denaturalization affected mainly members of the Muslim minority of Turkish ethnic origin. Approximately 60,000 individuals were deprived of their citizenship.[41] The Ministry of the Interior reported to the Greek Parliament in 2005 that 46,638 Muslims from Thrace and the Dodecanese Islands were deprived of their citizenship when they left the country between 1955 and 1998. The denaturalization allegedly took place in retaliation for Turkey's 1964 expulsion of 10,000 Greek citizens from Istanbul, ostensibly due to a deterioration of relations between Cyprus and Turkey.[42] The impugned article 19 was abolished in June 1998. A number of denaturalized Greek citizens requested that the Committee on Citizenship annul the decision that deprived them of their citizenship. Others requested acquisition of Greek citizenship through naturalization.[43] Article 19 was in violation, *inter alia*, of article 12, paragraph 4, of the International Covenant on Civil and Political Rights (ICCPR), ratified by Greece,[44] which provides that "[n]o one shall be arbitrarily deprived of the right to enter his own country." Greek officials have affirmed that only thirty individuals remain whose citizenship status has not been restored.[45] Officials also stated that only those who stayed in Greece were eligible to recover their lost citizenship. Some members of the Muslim minority claimed that this policy penalized Muslims who had moved abroad and subsequently acquired the citizenship of another country.

Greece's latest amendment to the Code of Nationality of 1955 to extend the acquisition of citizenship, traditionally limited to those born to a Greek mother or father (*jus sanguinis*), to those born in Greece (*jus soli*), provided that other conditions are met, has encountered legal challenges. In February 2011, the Council of State (the highest Administrative Court) declared unconstitutional articles 1, 14–21, and 24 of Law No. 3838/2010,[46] which grant Greek citizenship to foreigners who were born in Greece (*jus soli*) and were residents or students for a

---

[40] Stephanos Stavros, *Citizenship and the Protection of Minorities*, in GREECE IN A CHANGING EUROPE BETWEEN THE EUROPEAN INTEGRATION AND BALKAN DISINTEGRATION 119 (Kevin Featherstone & Kostas Ifantis eds., 1996).

[41] Hammarberg Report, *supra* note 6, ¶¶ 21–17.

[42] Nora Fisher Onar & Meric Ozgunec, *How Deep a Transformation? Europeanization of Greek and Turkish Minorities Policies*, 17 INTER. J. MINORITY & GROUP RIGHTS 115, 117 (2010).

[43] European Commission Against Racism and Intolerance (ECRI), *Second Report on Greece* 6, CRI (2000) 32 (Dec. 1999), http://hudoc.ecri.coe.int/XMLEcri/ENGLISH/Cycle_02/02_CbC_eng/02-cbc-greece-eng.pdf. ECRI was established by the Council of Europe as an independent human rights body in charge of issues related to racism and xenophobia.

[44] Law No. 2462/1997, *supra* note 37.

[45] Comments of the Greek Authorities, *in* Hammarberg Report, *supra* note 6, App. para. 4.

[46] Symvoulion Epikrateias [Council of State], Decision No. 350/2011 (Δ' Committee). A current bill submitted by the Ministry of Interior is seeking to abolish Law 3838/2010 based on the decision of the Council of State and because it constitutes a threat to national security and national cohesion. *See* http://www.hellenic parliament.gr/UserFiles/c8827c35-4399-4fbb-8ea6-aebdc768f4f7/Εγγραφο%20(7676995).pdf. See Greek Code of Nationality, *infra* note 145.

certain period. As the Council of State reasoned, Law No. 3838/2010 failed to take into account any additional substantive elements, especially that of the foreigner's ties to the Greek nation and his or her voluntary acceptance of Greek values, with a view to "attain[ing] Greek consciousness."[47] The Council noted that one of the objectives of the Constitution is the continuity of Greece as a nation through education, which aims to promote national and religious consciousness, and also through the nationality law, which provides for citizenship based on *jus sanguinis*. In this decision, the Council also declared unconstitutional the provisions of the same law that grant to foreigners of Greek descent legally residing in Greece the right to vote and to be elected in first-tier local elections. The decision was forwarded to the full assembly of the Council of State.[48]

B. Definition of 'Minority'

Notwithstanding the lack of a universal definition of "minority," two definitions have been developed that share similar features and have been cited extensively. The first definition was provided in 1930 by the PCIJ, and the second by Francesco Capotorti, Special Rapporteur of the United Nations Sub-Commission on Prevention of Discrimination and Protection of Minorities.

1. Permanent Court of International Justice & European Court of Human Rights

In its 1930 advisory opinion on the emigration of the Greco-Bulgarian community, the PCIJ defined a minority community as

> a group of persons living in a given country or locality having a race, religion, language and tradition in a sentiment of solidarity, with a view to preserving their traditions, maintaining their form of worship, ensuring the instruction and upbringing of their children in accordance with the spirit and tradition of their race and mutually assisting one another.[49]

In the 1935 *Minority Schools in Albania* case, the PCIJ reiterated this definition of a minority, and held that minorities exist as a matter of fact and not of law.[50] It also stated that the protection of minorities requires equality in law and in fact because special needs and equality in fact "are indeed closely interlocked, for there would be no true equality between a majority and a minority if the latter were deprived of its own institutions, and were consequently compelled to renounce that which constitutes the very essence of its being as a minority."[51]

A fundamental principle that evolved from the PCIJ case law is that the existence of communities is a question of historical fact and not of law, and consequently a state does not

---

[47] Symvoulion Epikrateias, Decision No. 350/2011, *supra* note 46.

[48] *Id.*

[49] Interpretation of the Convention Between Greece and Bulgaria Respecting Reciprocal Emigration, Advisory Opinion, PCIJ (1930), Series B, No. 17.33.

[50] Minority Schools in Albania, Advisory Opinion, PCIJ (Apr. 6, 1935), *in* 3 WORLD COURT REPORTS 484 (Mandley O. Hudson ed., 1932–1935).

[51] *Id.*

have the authority to determine whether a minority or minorities exist within its territory. More than sixty years after the *Minority Schools in Albania* decision, the ECHR in *Sidiropoulos v. Greece*[52] reaffirmed this principle by holding that the existence of minorities within a particular state is "a historical fact" and that a democratic state "had to tolerate and even protect and support [them] according to principles of international law."[53]

2. Capotorti's Definition

The definition coined by UN Special Rapporteur Francesco Capotorti is widely cited. In 1991, Capotorti defined a minority as

> [a] group numerically inferior to the rest of the population, in a non-dominant position, consisting of nationals of the State, possessing distinct ethnic, religious or linguistic characteristics and showing a sense of solidarity aimed at preserving those characteristics.[54]

The Special Rapporteur distinguished between the objective and subjective criteria of the notion of minority. Objective criteria include (a) numerical inferiority; (b) a non-dominant position; (c) the nationality of minority members; and (d) characteristics of the group, such as ethnic, religious, or linguistic characteristics. Subjective criteria include the "sense of solidarity" of the group with respect to maintaining and safeguarding its traditions, religion, language, and culture. According to Capotorti, the subjective element is a very important one. If a group meets the objective criteria, then nonrecognition of a particular group by the state does not free the state from its obligation to abide by international rules on minority protection.[55] In 1985, a similar definition was provided by Jules Deschenes, a member of the UN Sub-Committee on Prevention of Discrimination and Protection of Minorities.[56] The 1990 Copenhagen Document of the OSCE recognizes for the first time the concept of self-identification of minorities. Paragraph 32 states that "to belong to a national minority is a matter of a person's individual choice."[57]

Within the framework of the OSCE, the term "national minorities" is widely used to denote " a non dominant population that is a numerical minority within a State but that shares the same nationality/ethnicity as the population constituting a numerical majority in another, often

---

[52] Case of Sidiropoulos and Others v. Greece, *supra* note 30, para. 41.

[53] *Id.*

[54] CAPOTORTI, *supra* note 1, at 96.

[55] *Id. See also* ATHANASIA SPILIOPOULOU AKERMARK, JUSTIFICATIONS OF MINORITY PROTECTION IN INTERNATIONAL LAW 90 (1996).

[56] A minority is a "group of citizens of a State, constituting a numerical minority and in a non-dominant position in that State, endowed with ethnic, religious or linguistic characteristics which differ from those of the majority population, having a sense of solidarity with one another motivated, if only implicitly, by a collective will to survive and whose aim is to achieve equality with the majority in fact and law," JULES DESCHÊNES, PROMOTION, PROTECTION AND RESTORATION OF HUMAN RIGHTS AT THE NATIONAL, REGIONAL AND INTERNATIONAL LEVELS: PREVENTION OF DISCRIMINATION AND PROTECTION OF MINORITIES, *quoted in* U.N. Sub-Committee on Prevention of Discrimination and Protection of Minorities 1985 Meeting, U.N. Doc. E/CN.4/Sub.2/1985/31, para. 181.

[57] Copenhagen Document, *supra* note 1, para. 32.

neighboring or "kin" state."[58] The High Commissioner on National Minorities has also affirmed that the existence of a minority is a matter of fact and has adopted certain objective criteria to identify a minority, that is, a group of people with national, ethnic, or linguistic characteristics distinct from the majority that seeks to preserve and strengthen its identity.[59]

Based on the principles enunciated by the PCIJ, which have been further incorporated into current international legal instruments,[60] and the constituent elements of the definition of a minority, which require that a state must employ a set of objective and subjective criteria to reach a conclusion as to whether a particular minority exists within its territory,[61] one can argue that minorities exist in Greece, even though their precise number is not easily ascertained in the absence of specific demographic data due to statutory restrictions on the collection of data based on race, ethnicity, or religion. In identifying whether a particular group is a minority, the starting point is the self-identification of the group.[62] In addition, minorities have made their presence known, either collectively or individually, by instituting legal proceedings before domestic courts and the ECHR, after exhausting all domestic remedies; by the use of the media; and by bringing their claims to human rights organizations, including the OSCE.

3. Domestic Interpretations of 'Minority'

A 1930 report by the Ministry of Foreign Affairs grouped minorities into three categories depending on the degree of threat posed to Greece's national interests. In descending order (worst to least) these were: (a) Muslims of Western Thrace (whose status was already recognized by the Treaty of Lausanne of 1923), Slavophones in Macedonia, and Chams of Albanian origin in Thesprotia (the Chams had made more than twenty official protests to the League of Nations in Geneva; the report viewed this group as among the most dangerous because of their ties to neighboring states); (b) Koutsovlahi, Armenians (close to 80,000 came to Greece mostly after the Asia Minor Catastrophe, following the 1919–1922 war between Greece and Turkey), and Jews; and (c) the minority populations of Mount Athos, which included Russians, Bulgarians, and Romanian Monks.[63] At the same time, the Ministry of Foreign Affairs viewed the

---

[58] High Commissioner on National Minorities of the Organization for Security and Cooperation in Europe, Pamphlet 9, at 5, http://www.ohchr.org/Documents/Publications/GuideMinorities9en.pdf.

[59] *Id.*

[60] *See* ICCPR, *supra* note 37, art. 27; G.A. Res. 47/135, Declaration on the Rights of Persons Belonging to National or Ethnic, Religious or Linguistic Minorities (Dec. 18, 1992), *available at* http://www.oas.org/dil/ 1992%20Declaration%20on%20the%20Rights%20of%20Persons%20Belonging%20to%20National%20or%20Ethn ic,%20Religious%20and%20Linguistic.pdf; Convention on the Rights of the Child art. 30, Nov. 20, 1989, entry into force Sept. 2, 1990, 1577 U.N.T.S. 3, http://www2.ohchr.org/english/law/crc htm.

[61] *Minorities Under International Law*, OFFICE OF THE HIGH COMMISSIONER FOR HUMAN RIGHTS, UNITED NATIONS HUMAN RIGHTS, http://www.ohchr.org/EN/Issues/Minorities/Pages/internationallaw.aspx (last visited Sept. 28, 2012).

[62] STEVEN WHEATLEY, DEMOCRACY, MINORITIES AND INTERNATIONAL LAW 49 (2005).

[63] Lena Divani, *The Impact of the Minority System of the League of Nations in Greece: A Perspective of the Ministry of Foreign Affairs*, in KONSTANTINOS TSITSELIKIS & DIMITRIS CHRISTOPOULOS, TO MEINOTIKO PHAENOMENON STEN ELLADA [THE MINORITY PHENOMENON IN GREECE] 177 (1997) (in Greek). For a historical account of the Asia Minor Catastrophe, *see* DIMITRI PENTZOPOULOS, THE BALKAN EXCHANGE OF MINORITIES AND ITS IMPACT UPON GREECE 45 (1962).

Slavophones, who were claimed by Bulgaria and the former Yugoslavia for their own reasons of political expediency, as the biggest minority problem.[64]

Moreover, the 1951 census, which is the last census that used data based on ethnic and religious origin, indicated that at that time the following religious groups existed in Greece: 11,665 Muslims; 24,965 Catholics; 4,954 Protestants; and 6,325 Jews. In terms of linguistic minorities, there were 92,443 Turcophones; 41,017 Slavophones; 39,885 Vlachs; 22,736 Albanians; 18,671 Pomaks; and 7,429 Roma.[65]

Christos Rozakis, a former judge and former vice president of the ECHR, has stated that despite the fact of a mostly homogeneous Greek Orthodox population, "minorities do exist in Greece—of the kind recognized by international law—and even provoke a number of problems, which create tensions in their relationship with the majority."[66]

The legal literature identifies two main groups of minorities in Greece[67]—religious and linguistic.[68] Greece objects to the use of "minority religious groups" as "not politically correct" and suggests the use of "denominations other than Orthodox" instead.[69] Among the religious groups are a small number of Jews, whose religion is indeed officially recognized;[70] Catholics; Protestants; Old Calendarists; and Jehovah's Witnesses. Some data estimate the population of Old Calendarists at 500,000; Greek Catholics at 50,000; Protestants at 30,000; Jews at 5,000; and Muslims (with the exception of those in Western Thrace) at 100,000.[71] Among the linguistic groups are Arvanites; Albanians; Vlachs, whose language is Romanian; and Roma. Moreover, the Slavo-Macedonians have been described as both a linguistic and an ethnic group.[72]

Successive Greek governments have not recognized the Roma as a minority, with the exception of those who live in Western Thrace. Legislation and policy instruments consider them to be a "vulnerable social group," along with migrants. Roma amount to approximately

---

[64] *Id.* at 178.

[65] Stephanos Stavros, *The Legal Status of Minorities in Greece Today: The Adequacy of Their Protection in the Light of Current Human Rights Perceptions*, 13 J. MODERN GREEK STUDIES 1 (1995).

[66] Rozakis, *supra* note 31, at 98.

[67] Nicholas Sitaropoulos, *Freedom of Movement and the Right to a Nationality v. Ethnic Minorities: The Case of Ex Article 19 of the Greek Nationality Code*, 6 EURO. J. MIGRATION & L. 206 (2004). *See also* Rozakis, *supra* note 31, at 99.

[68] Stavros, *supra* note 65, at 9, 17; Christos Giakoumopoulos, *The Minority Phenomenon in Greece and the European Convention of Human Rights*, in TSITSELIKIS & CHRISTOPOULOS, *supra* note 63, at 45.

[69] Comments by the Greek Government on ECRI's Fourth Report Concerning Greece, *in* ECRI Report on Greece (Fourth Monitoring Cycle), App. (Sept. 15, 2009), http://www.coe.int/t/dghl/monitoring/ecri/country-by-country/greece/GRC-CbC-IV-2009-031-ENG.pdf.

[70] *Id.*

[71] Sitaropoulos, *supra* note 67, at 207.

[72] Rozakis, *supra* note 31, at 97, 98.

250,000–300,000, according to official estimates.[73] In Greece, the Roma who are mostly Muslims are referred to as Horahane Roma; they speak the Romani dialect and live mainly in the prefecture of Evros in southern Greece and in Komotini. This group of Roma is part of the Muslim minority pursuant to the Treaty of Lausanne. A number of Muslim Roma identify themselves with Turkey and stay connected with the Turkish Consulate General in Komotini, whereas others are loyal to Greece.[74] A large number of Roma are also concentrated in the suburbs of Athens and in the Peloponnese. The European Commission considers the Roma to be the "biggest ethnic minority in Europe, present in all 27 EU Member States," and numbering an estimated total of ten to twelve million. Most of them are EU citizens.[75] The EU has also paid particular attention to the Roma as a minority group within the EU territory. Moreover, the High Commissioner on National Minorities of the OSCE considers the Roma to fall within its remit following its 2000 *Report on the Roma and Sinti in the OSCE Area.*[76]

C. Individuals Who Self-Identify as Part of a 'Macedonian Minority'

Following the Greek-Bulgarian population exchange, most of the Slavophones settled in the areas of Florina and Kastoria.[77] In 1930, the Prefect of Florina estimated that those who spoke Slavic numbered close to 76,370. Another estimate was close to 60,000. Of those, 35,000 were viewed by the government as having anti-Greek sentiments. Another 25,000 belonged to a Bulgarian minority and, in the opinion of the government, were clearly acting against Greek interests and resisted being integrated with rest of the population.[78] At the end of World War II and the ensuing civil war of 1946–1949, most of the then remaining Bulgarians and Slavo-Macedonians left or were expelled from Greece.[79] The 1951 Greek census indicated that there were close to 40,000 Slavophones.[80] Rozakis has opined that most of the Slavophones have been integrated within Greek society with the exception of a few hard-core groups that live in small towns and mountainous villages and assert their ethnic identity as Slavo-Macedonians.[81] He also claims that after the emergence of the Former Yugoslav Republic of Macedonia (FYROM), such groups have been more aggressive and vocal in their assertions of a distinct "Macedonian minority."[82]

---

[73] Committee on the Elimination of Racial Discrimination, *Reports Submitted by States Parties Under Article 9 of the Convention:* Greece ¶ 7 (Mar. 27, 2008), U.N. Doc. CERD/C/GRC/16-19, http://www.unhcr.org/refworld/publisher,CERD,STATEPARTIESREP,,4aa7b7562,0.html.

[74] Alexandris, *supra* note 9, at 127.

[75] *About Us*, European Commission, http://ec.europa.eu/justice/mission/index_en.htm (last visited Sept. 25, 2012).

[76] Organization for Security and Co-operation in Europe, High Commissioner on National Minorities *Report on the Situation of Roma and Sinti in the OSCE Area* (2000), http://www.osce.org/hcnm/42063.

[77] For a historical background of the Slavo-Macedonians in Greece, *see* Anastasia Karakasidou, *Cultural Illegitimacy in Greece: The Slavo-Macedonian 'Non-Minority'*, *in* MINORITIES IN GREECE, *supra* note 3, at 122–64.

[78] VASILIS GOUNARIS, THE SLAVOPHONES OF MACEDONIA 99 (1977); TSITSELIKIS & CHRISTOPOULOS, *supra* note 63, at 73.

[79] Grigoriadis, *supra* note 32, at 25; *see also* GOUNARIS, *supra* note 78, at 106.

[80] Rozakis, *supra* note 31, at 98.

[81] *Id.* at 100.

[82] *Id.*

As stated previously, Greece denies that a distinct ethnic or linguistic minority exists in its territory by the name "Macedonian." It asserts that such claims are not based on the facts and moreover that the use of the word "Macedonian" creates uncertainty and misunderstanding among the 2.5 million residents of the Greek region of Macedonia.[83] Greece also alleges that they are being influenced by FYROM, a state that emerged in 1991 following the disintegration of the Yugoslav Republic. Since 1992, Greece has been in a dispute with FYROM over the use of the name "Macedonia" because it raises questions as to the Greek identity of the northern region of Greece, also named Macedonia; territorial claims on Greece made in FYROM's Constitution; and the use of the sun of Vergina in its flag, a symbol associated with Alexander the Great and his father Philip II.[84]

In 2008, Rainbow, the organization representing the "Macedonian minority" in Greece, demanded before the OSCE Human Dimension Implementation Meeting of the session on National Minorities to have the minority's linguistic rights enforced or recognized in Greece. Specifically, Rainbow asked that the minority's right to have their first and last names written in their own language be recognized by Greece. They alleged that their names had been converted to Greek during the 1920s and 1930s by Law No. 87/1936, which ordered Macedonians to change their Slavic names to Greek. In addition, they requested that the names of cities, towns, and villages that were replaced by Greek names by virtue of Decree No. 332/1926 be changed back to their language.[85] Moreover, the *Official Gazette of Greece* of July 15, 1927, contained an order requiring the deletion of all inscriptions written in Slavic from churches and forbidding the reading of the liturgy in Slavic.[86]

Greece has not ratified the European Charter for Regional or Minority Languages;[87] one could argue, however, that Greece's obligation to respect linguistic rights arises from article 27 of the ICCPR and the 1990 Copenhagen Document of the OSCE.

---

[83] Comments by the Greek Government on ECRI's Fourth Report Concerning Greece, *supra* note 69, at 62.

[84] FYROM joined the United Nations in 1993 under the provisional name of FYROM until the dispute with Greece is resolved. The United States recognized the country under the name of Republic of Macedonian in 1994 and has referred to it by its constitutional name, the Republic of Macedonia, since 2004. *A Guide to the United States' History of Recognition, Diplomatic and Consular Relations, by Country Since 1776: Macedonia*, DEPARTMENT OF STATE, OFFICE OF THE HISTORIAN, http://history.state.gov/countries/macedonia (last visited Sept. 28, 2012).

[85] Statement of Rainbow-Organization of the Macedonian Minority of Greece, 2008 OSCE Human Dimension Implementation Meeting Working Session 5: National Minorities (Oct. 2008). For a list of towns, cities, and other places that had their names changed, *see* HUMAN RIGHTS WATCH/HELSINKI, DENYING ETHNIC IDENTITY: THE MACEDONIANS OF GREECE 6 (1994), *available at* http://www.florina.org/news/helsinki_watch.pdf. The laws cited, Nos. 332/1926 and 87/1936, could not be found in the database of the *Gazette of Greece*. The list of towns and cities is included in the Appendix of the above-referenced report by Human Rights Watch/Helsinki.

[86] HUMAN RIGHTS WATCH/HELSINKI, *supra* note 85, at 6. The *Gazette* of July 15, 1927, containing an order to delete all inscriptions could not be located.

[87] European Charter for Regional or Minority Languages, C.E.T.S. No. 148 (1992), http://conventions.coe.int/treaty/Commun/QueVoulezVous.asp?NT=148&CM=1&CL=ENG. Greece has neither signed nor ratified the Convention. *See* Chart of Ratifications, http://conventions.coe.int/treaty/Commun/ChercheSig.asp?NT=148&CM=1&DF=&CL=ENG (last updated Sept. 28, 2012).

Greece, while arguing that there is no "Macedonian minority" within its borders, characterizes the traditional festivities and cultural events that take place in the region of Florina as an "integral part of the local population's culture," and takes the position that these festivities and events "include a small group of Greek citizens, who also speak a Slavic dialect and who live in this area."[88] One could argue that international law on minorities does not require a minimum number to form a minority[89] and that such festivities could be deemed as expressions of the existence of an ethnic/linguistic minority, which Greece has undertaken to respect and protect based on its ICCPR and OSCE commitments. The *Areios Pagos* (Supreme Court of Greece), however, has stated that the OSCE commitments are not legally binding.[90]

D. Case Law

The first case referenced below concerns the right of an ethnic organization to register under the name of "Home of Macedonian Civilization." The ECHR has recognized that there is a wide "margin of appreciation" given to member states when they impose restrictions on rights on the grounds of public interest and security. However, even the margin of appreciation falls under the supervision of the ECHR and states do not enjoy unfettered power when curtailing freedom of association on the grounds of public interest and security.

In the case of *Sidiropoulos and Others v. Greece*,[91] the applicants, citizens of Florina in northern Greece who claimed to be of Macedonian ethnic origin and to have a "Macedonian national consciousness," decided to establish an association, the "Home of Macedonian Civilization." The association's stated objectives included the cultural, intellectual, and artistic development of its members and the citizens of Florina, promotion and development of cooperation and solidarity among them, and protection of the region's natural and cultural environment.

The competent court of Florina refused to register the association on the grounds that, according to newspaper accounts, some of its members were engaged in promoting the idea that there is a "Macedonian minority" in Greece and that its representatives participated in the Copenhagen Meeting of the Conference of the Human Dimension of the Conference on Security and Co-operation in Europe in June 1990, where they expressed the view that there is a "Macedonian minority" in Greece. The Court of Appeals upheld the decision of the lower court on the grounds that the applicants intended to dispute the Greek identity of Macedonia and to undermine Greece's territorial integrity. The applicants appealed to the Supreme Court, which upheld the Court of Appeals' judgment.[92] The applicants applied to the then-existing European Commission of Human Rights and argued that the Greek court's refusal to register the association violated their right to freedom of association as enshrined in article 11 of the European Convention for the Protection of Human Rights and Fundamental Freedoms

---

[88] Comments of the Greek Authorities, *in* Hammarberg Report, *supra* note 6, App. para. 2.

[89] CAPOTORTI, *supra* note 1, at 12.

[90] Decision of Areios Pagos [Supreme Court], No. 4/2005, in plenum, http://www.areiospagos.gr/ nomologia/apofaseis_DISPLAY.asp?cs=vgNmpsPAM16MMv.

[91] Case of Sidiropoulos and Others v. Greece, *supra* note 30.

[92] Decision of Areios Pagos, No. 1448/2009, Δ Civil Section, http://www.areiospagos.gr/en/INDEX.htm.

(ECHRFF). The ECHR examined whether the interference of the courts with the applicants' right to form an association was justified based on law, which it answered in the positive. Then it examined whether the interference had a legitimate aim, and it accepted that given the political turmoil in Greece's relations with the FYROM, the interference aimed to safeguard Greece's national security. In examining the last standard, that the interference must be necessary in a democratic society, the Court stated that

> [t]erritorial integrity, national security and public order were not threatened by the activities of an association whose aim was to promote a region's culture, even supposing that it also aimed partly to promote the culture of a minority; the existence of minorities and different cultures in a country was a historical fact that a "democratic society" had to tolerate and even protect and support according to the principles of international law.[93]

Furthermore, it asserted that the aims of the association to preserve and promote the traditions of the Florina area "were perfectly clear and legitimate." The ECHR also noted that the Greek courts had the power to dissolve the association after its establishment, if its subsequent aims were different from those stated in its memorandum. As of July 2011, the "Home of Macedonian Civilization" had not yet been registered and its case was pending before the Supreme Court.[94]

The second case involved a political party, *Ouranio Toxo* (Rainbow), established in 1994, which participated in elections with the stated objective of defending the interests of the "Macedonian minority." In 1995, *Ouranio Toxo* established its headquarters in Florina and affixed the sign of the party's name in Macedonian. The local citizens were provoked by the sign, which served as a reminder of the civil war in Greece, and damaged the headquarters. The police removed the sign. The government justified the removal of the sign because of the social turmoil it would provoke among the residents of Florina. *Ouranio Toxo* applied to the ECHR, alleging a violation of article 11 of the Convention. The ECHR issued its judgment in the case of *Ouranio Toxo and Others v. Greece* on October 20, 2005, and observed *inter alia* that *Ouranio Toxo* was a lawfully established political party and that placing a sign with the party's name written in the Slavic alphabet as Vinozito could not be perceived as a threat to public order. The ECHR acknowledged that the word "Vinozito" rekindled hostile feelings among the local population. The Court said that the danger of creating friction within the community is not sufficient to justify interference with the right of association by public authorities.[95] The just satisfaction awarded by the ECHR in the amount of €35,245 (approximately US$45,469) was paid in full by Greece on May 2, 2006. Greece undertook a number of general measures, including the dissemination of the judgment to the Ministries of Justice and Public Order, and the Head of Police, and the translation of the case into Greek by the Legal Council of State. The Supreme Court forwarded the judgment to all judicial authorities and the competent judicial authorities in Florina. To instill a sense of security in citizens, new police orders provide for

---

[93] Case of Sidiropoulos and Others v. Greece, *supra* note 30, para. 41.

[94] Minority Rights Group International, State of the World's Minorities and Indigenous Peoples 2011 – Greece (July 6, 2011), *available at* http://www.unhcr.org/refworld/docid/4e16d3732a.html.

[95] Ouranio Toxo and Others v. Greece, App. No. 74989/01, Eur. Ct. H.R. (Oct. 2005), ECHR 2005-X (extracts).

twenty-four-hour security surveillance of sensitive targets, such as the premises of political parties or those of local organizations in order to avoid acts of aggression.[96]

III. Status of Minorities in Greece Based on Treaties Under the League of Nations System

A. Historical and Legal Framework

1. Treaty of Sèvres

As a newly established nation in 1830, Greece assumed its first obligation toward its minorities by virtue of the 1st Protocol of London of 1830, which established Greece's birth as a new nation. The 1st Protocol also secured the religious, civil, and political equality of all inhabitants without any discrimination.[97] The Treaty of London of 1864 provided for the protection of religious freedom of Catholics in the Ionian Islands and for political and civil equality of people of different religions and denominations.[98] Article 8 of the Agreement of Constantinople on Greek-Turkish borders, which was concluded in 1881, guaranteed religious freedom and civil rights to Muslim inhabitants of the Epirus and Thessalia areas of Greece.[99] Religious protection was extended to Muslim inhabitants of the new lands pursuant to the Athens Agreements of 1913 between Greece and Turkey.[100]

The Treaty of Sèvres on Minorities of August 10, 1920,[101] was agreed to by the victorious allied powers (Greece, the British Empire, Italy, Japan, and France), and the Ottoman Empire. The Sèvres Peace Treaty of the same date ended the Ottoman Empire and established modern Turkey. The Peace Treaty was later renounced by Turkey and was superseded by the Treaty of Lausanne.

The Treaty of Sèvres on Minorities was ratified by Greece on September 29, 1923, and published in the *Official Gazette of Greece*.[102] It established a legal framework for the

---

[96] Council of Europe, Committee of Ministers, Resolution (CM)/ResDH(2011)218, at 96 (adopted Dec. 2, 2011), https://wcd.coe.int/ViewDoc.jsp?id=1882433&Site=&BackColorInternet=B9BDEE&BackColor Intranet=FFCD4F&BackColorLogged=FFC679#P3763_232720.

[97] Protocol No. 1 of February 3, 1830 on the Independence of Greece, available on the website of the Foreign Ministry of Greece, *at* http://www.mfa.gr//images/docs/diethneis_symvaseis/1830_london_protocol.doc (in French).

[98] Treaty of London of March 29, 1864, *available at* http://www.mfa.gr/images/docs/diethneis_symvaseis/1864_london_treaty.doc.

[99] Convention of Konstantinople of 1881 on the Greek-Turkish Borders, *available at* http://www.mfa.gr//images/docs/diethneis_symvaseis/1881_constantinople_convention.doc (in French).

[100] Peace Convention of Athens, Nov. 14, 1913, *available at* http://www.mfa.gr//images/docs/diethneis_symvaseis/1913_athens_convention.doc (in French).

[101] Treaty Concerning the Protection of Minorities in Greece (Treaty of Sèvres on Minorities), Aug. 10, 1920, 28 L.N.T.S. 243, *reprinted in* 15 AM. J. INTL'L L. 161 (Supp. 1921).

[102] E.K.E.D., A: 311, Oct. 30, 1923, http://www.et.gr/index.php?option=com_wrapper&view= wrapper&Itemid=104&lang=el.

protection of minorities in Greece under the League of Nations.[103]   Currently, however, the Greek government deems the Treaty of Sèvres as no longer valid.[104]

The Legislative Decree of August 25, 1923, on Ratification of the Lausanne Agreement of Peace,[105] recognized the validity of the No. XVI Protocol to the Treaty of Lausanne relating to the Treaty of Sèvres on Minorities. In the 1950s, the United Nations' *Study of the Legal Validity of the Undertakings Concerning Minorities*,[106] which examined whether certain agreements on minorities were still binding and survived the events of the Second World War, the dissolution of the League of Nations, and the birth of the United Nations system, held that the dissolution of the League of Nations and the impact of the war did not bring about an *ipso facto* termination of the treaties executed under the League of Nations. In reviewing each treaty separately, the study stated that all of them, including the Treaty of Sèvres, were abrogated based on the change of circumstances (*rebus sic stantibus*) principle. Only the Treaty of Lausanne and an agreement between Finland and Sweden on the Aland Islands survived. The findings of the UN General Secretariat are not conclusive or accepted by all scholars, however.[107]

Domestically, the status of the Treaty of Sèvres is disputed. The Greek judiciary and the legal literature still refer to the Treaty of Sèvres on Minorities of 1920 by virtue of which Greece undertook obligations to respect its minorities living within its much expanded territory, gained in 1919.[108] A number of courts have invoked and applied the ratification law and argued that it is still in force in the absence of a later law abolishing the ratification law.[109] Based on the dualist theory of international law that existed in Greece prior to 1975, some have argued that, irrespective of the status of the Treaty of Sèvres, the ratification law continued to exist at the international level until 1975, when the new Constitution adopted the monist theory.[110]

As late as 1994, the Supreme Court held that the Treaty was still in force as national law, because it was ratified by a law. However, those provisions of the Treaty that govern the same rights and freedoms as the ECHRFF are superseded by the European Convention, as it was adopted later in time. On the other hand, provisions of the Treaty of Sèvres, which are *lex*

---

[103] Treaty of Sèvres on Minorities, *supra* note 101.

[104] Information provided to the author by the Greek Ministry of Foreign Affairs (2011).

[105] Ratification of the Treaty of Sèvres, E.K.E.D., A:238, Aug. 25, 1923.

[106] Study of the Legal Validity of the Undertakings Concerning Minorities, U.N. Doc. E/CN.4/367 (1950).

[107] *See* SPILIOPOULOU AKERMARK, *supra* note 55, at 121–22.

[108] For example, the Treaty of Sèvres was cited as relevant Greek law in *Case of the Canea Catholic Church*, which initially arose in the District Court of Canea, reached the Supreme Court of Greece, and eventually was decided by the European Court of Human Rights. Case of the Canea Catholic Church v. Greece, App. No. 143/1996/762/963, Eur. Ct. H.R. (Dec. 16, 1997), http://hudoc.echr.coe.int/sites/eng/pages/search.aspx?i=001-58124.

[109] Konstantinos Tsitselikis, The International and European Status for the Protection of the Linguistic Minority Rights and the Greek Legal Order 326 (1996).

[110] *Id.* at 327.

specialis in relation to the European Convention and are neither provided for there nor in conflict with it, are still in force.[111]

Based on the above reasoning of the Supreme Court, the provisions of the Treaty of Sèvres pertaining to freedom of religion for all inhabitants of Greece (which at that time included Bulgarians and Jews, without distinction of birth, nationality, language, race, or religion) and the provisions related to enjoyment of all civil and political rights of all inhabitants have been superseded by the European Convention.

In two judgments, issued in 2001 and 2003 respectively, the Council of State held that the Treaty of Sèvres remains valid.[112]

2. Legal Provisions on Minorities

The object of the Treaty of Sèvres on Minorities was to guarantee protection of all minorities living in Greece at that time, including the population of the newly annexed Western Thrace.[113] On the basis of the Treaty, Greece granted citizenship without any formality to Bulgarians, Turks, and Albanians who were living in the territories transferred to Greece, subsequent to January 1, 1913. The provision on religious minorities, along with other provisions that ensured religious freedom and granted equal rights to all inhabitants, has superior status because it was recognized as "fundamental law." It is followed by a declaration that "the stipulations contained in articles 2 to 8 of this chapter shall be considered as fundamental law and . . . no law, regulation, or official action shall conflict or interfere with these stipulations, nor shall any law, regulation, or official action prevail over them."

Article 8 of the Treaty of Sèvres, relating to minorities, is of particular significance with respect to the issue under discussion:

> Greek nationals who belong to racial, religious or linguistic minorities shall enjoy the same treatment and security in law and in fact as the other Greek nationals. In particular, they shall have an equal right to establish, manage and control, at their own expense, charitable, religious, and social institutions, schools and other educational establishments, with the right to use their own language and to exercise their religion therein.

In September 1924, the Kalfov-Politis Protocol, signed by the Bulgarian and Greek representatives at the League of Nations, placed the Bulgarian minority in Greece under the protection of the League of Nations.[114] Under the Protocol, Greece assumed the obligation to safeguard the rights of its Bulgarian minority in Greece in accordance with the Treaty of Sèvres. On January 25, 1925, Greece announced that it would not implement the Protocol. The signing

---

[111] Supreme Court decision No. 360/1994, *cited in id.*

[112] Symvoulion Epikrateias 1333/2001, para. 7, *and* 466/2003, para. 6, *cited in* YANNIS KTISTAKIS, IEROS NOMOS TOU ISLAM KAI MOUSOULMANOI ELLINES POLITES [SHARIA LAW AND MUSLIM GREEK CITIZENS] 96 (2006).

[113] Treaty of Sèvres on Minorities, *supra* note 101. *See also* KTISTAKIS, *supra* note 112, at 95.

[114] Iakovos D. Michailidis, *Minority Rights and Educational Problems in Greek Interwar Macedonia: The Case of the Primer 'Abecedar,'* 14(2) J. MOD. GREEK STUDIES 329 (1996).

of the Protocol by Greece has been interpreted as an admission that the Slavophones in Macedonia were of Bulgarian descent.[115] The Protocol was never ratified by the Greek Parliament to the dismay of the League of Nations, which subsequently released Greece from its obligations arising from the Protocol and asked Greece to respond to a questionnaire regarding the measures taken with respect to its minorities.[116] Greece promised that it would assist its Slavophone minorities and would open schools and print books in their language. As far as religious freedom, the Slavophones would be free to hire Slavophone priests for church services. From that time on, Greece started calling the minority "Slavophones" or "Macedonian-slavs" to minimize the minority's ties with Bulgaria.[117] In implementation of Greece's obligation, the *Abecedar*, a school book for teaching grammar written in the Latin alphabet, was prepared in 1925 by the Greek government to be used for Slavic-speaking Greeks. Though intended as a primer for the Slavophones, the *Abecedar* was never distributed.[118]

3. Treaty of Lausanne & Creation of the Muslim Minority in Western Thrace

The legal status of the Muslim minority is determined on the basis of the Treaty of Peace with Turkey Signed at Lausanne on July 23, 1923, at the end of the Lausanne Peace Conference.[119] The Treaty was signed between the British Empire, France, Italy, Japan, Greece, Romania, and the Serb-Croat-Slovene State on one part, and Turkey on the other. The Peace Conference also included the Convention and Protocol on the Exchange of Greek and Turkish Populations concluded at Lausanne on January 30, 1923.[120] In the aftermath of the Greco-Turkish War in 1922, an exchange of population between Greece and Turkey was carried out pursuant to article 1 of the Lausanne Convention on the Exchange of Greek and Turkish Populations,[121] which states that "there shall take place a compulsory exchange of Turkish nationals of the Greek Orthodox Religion established in Turkish territory, and of Greek nationals of the Moslem religion established in the Greek territory." Muslims from Crete were also included, even though their affiliation with the receiving country was questionable.[122]

One of the key objectives of the Lausanne Treaty was to protect the rights of the Greek Orthodox minority in Turkey and the rights of the Turkish minority in Western Thrace.[123] These

---

[115] *Id.* at 329.

[116] Lena Divani, Ellada Kai Meionotetes, To Systema Tes Diethnous Prostasias Tes Koinonias Ton Ethnon [Greece and Minorities: The System of Protection Under the League of Nations] 324–25(1995). *See also* Michailidis, *supra* note 114, at 340.

[117] Michailidis, *supra* note 114, at 323.

[118] *Id.* at 180, 324.

[119] Lausanne Treaty, *supra* note 12.

[120] Convention and Protocol on the Exchange of Greek and Turkish Populations, Jan. 30, 1923, *in* 18 Am. J. Int'l L. 84 (1924).

[121] Convention on the Exchange of Greek and Turkish Populations, *id.*, art. 1. *See also* Dimitri Pentzopoulos, The Balkan Exchange of Minorities and Its Impact Upon Greece 68 (1962).

[122] Michael Barutciski, *Lausanne Revisited Population Exchanges in International Law and Policy*, *in* 12 Crossing the Aegean, *supra* note 9, at 30.

[123] Rozakis, *supra* note 31, at 103.

populations were exempted from the exchange as provided in article 2 of the Convention on the Exchange of Greek and Turkish Populations:

> The following persons shall not be included in the exchange provided for in Article 1:
> (a)   The Greek inhabitants of Constantinople; and
> (b)   The Moslem inhabitants of Western Thrace.

Furthermore, article 2 defined the Greek inhabitants and the Muslim inhabitants for purposes of the Convention. It stated that all Greeks who were already established prior to October 30, 1918, within the areas under the Prefecture of the City of Constantinople, as defined by the law of 1912, shall be deemed Greek inhabitants of Constantinople. As far as the Moslems living in Western Thrace, article 2 elaborated that "all Moslems established in the region to the east of the frontier line laid down in 1913 by the Treaty of Bucharest shall be considered as Moslem inhabitants of Western Thrace."[124]

Consequently, the above populations who remained in Greece and Turkey, respectively, were put into the minority protection system under the League of Nations.[125] There are no accurate accounts of the number of Muslims who stayed in Thrace and the number of Greeks who stayed in Constantinople (Istanbul). According to some sources, the numbers were almost equal—close to 130,000.[126] Alexandris cites 110,000 Greek Orthodox in Istanbul.[127] The Lausanne Mixed Commission issued 106,000 permits to Muslims in Thrace who became Greek citizens.[128]

The compulsory exchange of population that was carried out on the basis of religion was designed to create homogeneous nation-states and reduce to some extent the presence of minorities in both states.[129] Close to 360,000 Muslim Greeks left Greece to settle in Turkey and by 1925, between 125,000 and 190,000 Greeks (Rum Orthodox) had left Turkey. In addition, Greece received close to 1.2 million persons who fled Turkey after the Asia Minor Catastrophe.[130] When the Dodecanese Islands were annexed to Greece, there were close to 5,000 Muslims who were Greek citizens on the islands of Cos and Rodos. These Muslims are not considered to be a minority.

Today, the Muslim minority, even though its members are Greek citizens, maintains relations and political ties with the kin state, Turkey.[131] According to official estimates,[132] the

---

[124] Convention on the Exchange of Greek and Turkish Populations, *supra* note 120, art. 2.

[125] Barutciski, *in* CROSSING THE AEGEAN, *supra* note 9, at 30.

[126] Baskin Oran, *The Story of Those Who Stayed, Lessons from Articles 1 and 2 of the 1923 Convention, in* 12 CROSSING THE AEGEAN, *supra* note 9, at 100.

[127] Alexandris, *supra* note 9, at 116.

[128] *Id.* at 122.

[129] DIMITRI PENTZOPOULOS, BALKAN EXCHANGE OF MINORITIES AND ITS IMPACT UPON GREECE 131 (1962).

[130] *Id.* at 48.

[131] Based on the author's observations, many Turkish students opt to study in universities in Turkey, rather than in Greece.

minority in Thrace consists of approximately 100,000 citizens compared to 362,000 of the rest of the Muslim population. Pursuant to the 2011 census conducted by the Statistical Service of Greece, the legal population of Greece (those who are legally registered in local registries) amounts to 9,903,268.[133] Western Thrace (comprising the regions of Xanthi, Rodopi, and Evros) has a legally registered population of 365,816. The Greek Orthodox minority population in Turkey has been reduced from 120,000 in 1930 to approximately 4,000 in 2007, with fewer than 300 living as permanent residents on the islands of Gokceada/Imvros and Bozcaada/Tenedos.[134] No statistics regarding the Muslim minority are available because of restrictions on the processing of personal data on ethnicity or religion. The 2001 census indicated that Western Thrace had a population of 355,571. Of those, 85,000 were registered as belonging to the Muslim minority.[135]

B. Treatment of the Muslim Minority

The Greek dictatorship that assumed power in 1967 applied the principle of reciprocity restrictively, especially in the areas of education of minorities and the *vakfs*.[136] Moreover, the regime subjected the minority to administrative harassment (*katastaltika metra*), for example, by delaying their applications for drivers' licenses. As stated above, the denaturalization of approximately 50,000 ethnic Turks stands out because of its adverse impact on a large number of ethnic Turks in Thrace.[137]

---

[132] Greece is among several other EU countries (Belgium, France, Germany, Netherlands, and Sweden) that do not collect data on the ethnic, religious, or linguistic aspects of their populations, because such a declaration would contravene the law on personal data protection. Processing of personal data related to an ethnic, cultural, or religious minority must be in conformity with article 8 of the Charter of Fundamental Rights, Convention No. 108 for the Protection of Individuals with Regard to Automatic Processing of Personal Data, http://conventions.coe.int/Treaty/en/Treaties/Html/108.htm, and Directive 95/46/EC on the Protection of Individuals with Regard to the Processing of Personal Data and on the Free Movement of Such Data, http://eur-lex.europa.eu/LexUriServ/LexUriServ.do?uri=OJ:L:1995:281:0031:0050:EN:PDF. For more information on the tension arising from carrying out a census and asking people about their affiliation with minorities, *see* E.U. Network of Independent Experts on Fundamental Rights, Thematic Comment No. 3: The Protection of Minorities in the European Union, at 12 (Apr. 25, 2005).

[133] Press Release, Greek Statistical Service, Census of 2011 (July 31, 2012), http://www.statistics.gr/portal/page/portal/ESYE/BUCKET/General/NWS_CENSUS_310712_GR.pdf (in Greek).

[134] Van Koufoudakis, *International Law and Minority Protection: The Fate of the Greeks of Imbros and Tenedos*, 19(4) MEDITERRANEAN QUARTERLY (2008). *See also* KONSTANTINOS TSITSELIKIS, THE MINORITY PROTECTION SYSTEM IN GREECE AND TURKEY BASED ON THE TREATY OF LAUSANNE (1923): A LEGAL OVERVIEW 4 (June 11, 2008); Steven Stavros Skenderis, Note and Comment, *The Ethnic Greeks of Turkey: The Present Situation of the Greek minority and Turkey's Human Rights Obligations Under International law*, 16 ST. THOMAS L. REV. 551 (2004).

[135] *Greek Statistical Service*, GENERAL SECRETARIAT OF THE NATIONAL STATISTICAL SERVICE OF GREECE, http://www.statistics.gr (in Greek; last visited Oct. 1, 2012).

[136] Konstantinos Tsitselikis, *Reciprocity as a Regulatory Pattern for the Treatment of the Turkish Muslim Minority of Greece*, in RECIPROCITY: GREEK AND TURKISH MINORITIES LAW, RELIGION AND POLITICS 79 (Samim Akgonul ed., 2008).

[137] Initially, the measure was intended to affect Communists during the Civil War in Greece and, after 1960, it was used against the Turkish-speaking Muslims. For more information, *see* Sitaropoulos, *supra* note 67, at 215.

Greece's policy vis-à-vis its minority took a positive turn in the aftermath of minority protests and intercommunal strife in Thrace that occurred in 1989/1990.[138] A number of sources indicate that this change in minority relations followed then-Prime Minister Konstantinos Mitsotakis' visit to Thrace in May 1991,[139] where he recognized officially that the Muslim minority in Thrace is composed of three ethnic groups with distinct characteristics that must be respected pursuant to the Treaty of Lausanne and Greek law.[140] A new policy was adopted that was designed to cease all suppressive measures imposed until then[141] and to ensure that, as stated by Mitsotakis, all the members of the minority enjoyed equality and equal protection under the law.[142]

During the ensuing years, Greece's adoption of the 1993 electoral law (Presidential Decree 353/1993 art. 87, para. 10) requiring 3% of electoral votes for the participation of a party or as a member in Parliament was perceived as in effect precluding the election of independent candidates from the Muslim minority, although such a requirement applied to every party. On the other hand, in 1995, Greece took several steps to facilitate the daily lives of the Muslim minority through the simple measure of facilitating the issuance of driver's licenses[143] and by removing other restrictions, including the physical barrier that restricted the movement of Pomaks and the restrictions on entry and movement of Greek citizens to the so-called Controlled Zone; it also created new roads that ended the isolation of the Pomak villages.[144] These actions culminated in the abolition of the contentious article 19 of the Citizenship Code in 1998,[145] due to increased pressure and protests from human rights organizations.

---

[138] DIA ANAGNOSTOU & ANNA TRANDAFYLLIDOU, REGIONS, MINORITIES AND EUROPEAN INTEGRATION: A CASE STUDY ON MUSLIMS IN WESTERN THRACE, GREECE (Hellenic Foundation for European and Foreign Policy (ELIAMEP), undated), http://www.eliamep.gr/wp-content/uploads/en/2006/05/Case_study_report_Thrace.pdf.

[139] MANOLIS KOTTAKIS, THRAKE HE MEIONOTETA SIMERA [THRACE, THE MINORITY TODAY] 35 (2000). *See also* TASOS KOSTOPOULOS, TO MAKEDONIKO TES THRAKES [THE MACEDONIAN ISSUE OF THRACE] 148 (2009).

[140] Similar promises were made by then Prime Minister George Papandreou during his February 18, 2011, visit to Western Thrace, where he emphasized his government's steadfast support of the principles of equality and nondiscrimination. Apostolos Papapostolou, *Papandreou Tours Thrace and Visits Muslim Minority*, GREEK REPORTER (Feb. 18, 2011), http://greece.greekreporter.com/2011/02/18/papandreou-tours-thrace-visits-muslim-minority.

[141] A 2008 circular from the Secretary of the Service of Foreign and Minority Schools ordered that all school celebrations of the national holidays of October 28, March 25, and November 17 be conducted only in Greek and not in Turkish due to the lack of equivalent poems in Turkish. KOSTOPOULOS, *supra* note 139, at 251.

[142] *Id.* at 149. This is also supported by Meinardus, *supra* note 3, at 92. *See also* ANAGNOSTOU & TRANDAFYLLIDOU, *supra* note 138.

[143] KOTTAKIS, *supra* note 139. Cutting bureaucracy was one of the key messages of Papandreou's visit to Western Thrace on February 18, 2011, who called red tape "the oppressor of Christians and Muslims alike" and promised to introduce driving license tests in Turkish. *Greece: PM Visits Minority Village, Promises to Settle Problems*, ISLAM IN EUROPE (Feb. 20, 2011), http://islamineurope.blogspot.com/2011/02/greece-pm-visits-muslim-minority.html.

[144] KOSTOPOULOS, *supra* note 139, 152–53. *See also* Grigoriadis, *supra* note 32; ANAGNOSTOU & TRIANDAFYLLIDOU, *supra* note 138, at 104.

[145] Greek Code of Nationality, as codified by Legislative Decree 3370/1955, *as amended.* The latest amendment was by Law No. 3838, 2010, E.K.E.D., part A, No. 49, 2010, *available at* http://www.et.gr/index.php?option=com_wrapper&view=wrapper&Itemid=108&lang=el (in Greek; click on Law 3838/2010).

1. Denial of Ethnic Identity

In the early 1950s, Greece used the term "Turkish" in reference to the Muslim minority in Thrace, following an order by the Prime Minister.[146] Hence, minority schools were referred to as Turkish schools and the Turkish language became obligatory for all segments of the Muslim minority, including Pomaks, who developed closer ties with ethnic Turks and Turkey as a result.[147] That policy lasted only a short time. In the aftermath of the mistreatment of the Greek minority in Istanbul in 1955, the strife between Greek Cypriots and Turkish Cypriots in Cyprus in 1963, and the military takeover of power in 1967, Greece ceased referring to the Muslim minority as Turkish.[148]

Denial of their ethnic identity continues to be a contentious issue between the ethnic Turks who are Greek citizens and Greece. The efforts of the ethnic Turks to be recognized as an ethnic minority have not been successful thus far. In the early 1990s, the first applications filed before the ECHR by minority organizations were not successful because most of them were found inadmissible on the grounds of non-exhaustion of domestic remedies or were deemed manifestly ill-founded.[149] One such case was the *Sadik case*, which highlights Greece's response to such demands. Dr. Ahmet Sadik, a distinguished doctor and Turkish nationalist was elected twice as an independent to the Greek Parliament. As a candidate in general elections from the area of Rodopi, Dr. Sadik claimed that he was a member of the Turkish minority. He was convicted by the Greek criminal courts for engaging in actions against the public order and inciting the local citizens to commit violence. He was jailed for three months. In the aftermath of Sadik's conviction, a great deal of turmoil erupted in the Komotini region of Western Thrace, which resulted in the destruction of 400 Muslim-owned shops and buildings.[150] The ECHR declined to hear the case due to the lack of exhaustion of local remedies.[151]

---

[146] A small 1956 study of the Muslim minority states that the Muslim minority is referred to as Turkish due to its use of the Turkish language, and because Turkey expressly and repeatedly requested that the term "Turkish" to be used. In order to maintain positive ties with Turkey, the Greek government agreed to this request. K.G. ANDREADOU, THE MUSLIM MINORITY OF WESTERN THRACE 4 (Association of Macedonian Studies, Thessaloniki, 1956).

[147] *Id*. The study referenced above includes an order issued by the General Administrator of Thrace to the mayors and presidents of municipalities of the Thrace, to comply with the Government's directive to replace any usage of the word "Muslim" with the word "Turk" or "Turkish" and to ensure that the sign on the village of Aratos, which bears the words "Muslim School," and any other sign to this effect be replaced with the word "Turkish." *Id*. at 10.

[148] ANAGNOSTOU & TRIANDAFYLLIDOU, *supra* note 138.

[149] Evangelia Psychogiopoulou, *The European Court of Human Rights in Greece: Litigation, Rights Protection and Vulnerable Groups*, *in* THE EUROPEAN COURT OF HUMAN RIGHTS AND THE RIGHTS OF MARGINALISED INDIVIDUALS AND MINORITIES IN NATIONAL CONTEXT at 127 (Dia Anagnostou & Evangelia Psychogiopoulou eds., 2010).

[150] Onar & Ozgunec, *supra* note 42, at 125.

[151] The *Sadik* case and the later case of *Beis v. Greece* were influential in amending article 15, paragraph 2 of the 1975 Constitution. Article 15 stipulates the obligatory and free broadcast of Parliament's debates and also the free broadcast of pre-election campaign messages of political parties. Based on the *Beis* case, article 94, para. 4 guarantees the compulsory enforcement of court decisions against the State, local self-government, and legal entities

2. Violation of the Right of Association

The right of all Greeks to form a nonprofit union or association is guaranteed by the Greek Constitution, which prohibits the exercise of this right to be made subject to a prior authorization.[152] Pursuant to the Greek Civil Code, at least twenty persons are necessary to form a nonprofit association, and such an association acquires legal personality upon its registration in the public register of the court of first instance of the place where the association has its headquarters. The application must be accompanied by certain documents, including a memorandum that must specify, *inter alia*, the object, name, and place of the association. Upon review of the documentation provided, the court may issue a decision to register the association. The court also has the right to dissolve the association for a number of reasons, including the ground that the association pursues aims different from those stated in its memorandum.[153]

In addition, Greece is obliged to respect the right of association of article 11 of the ECHRFF, which guarantees the right of association to every individual, albeit with no specific reference to minorities.[154] However, applicants, members of a minority, can find effective protection of their right of association based on the nondiscrimination principle enshrined in article 14 of the Convention. Article 14 encompasses indirect discrimination and affirmative action measures.[155]

Moreover, the OSCE Copenhagen Document, which guarantees minorities the right to establish and maintain organizations and associations in the countries where they live and the right to participate in international nongovernmental organizations,[156] provides for the right of association.

The cases of *Bekir-Ousta and Others v. Greece* (2007), *Emin and Others v. Greece* (2008), and *Tourkiki Enosi Xanthis and Others v. Greece* (2008) share common features. They involve state interference with the right of association, as protected by the Greek Constitution and article 11 of the ECHRFF. Specifically, the applicants, all members of the Muslim minority and Greek citizens, attempted to establish Turkish rather than Muslim associations in Greece. The Greek courts rejected their applications mainly on the grounds that the Treaty of Lausanne

---

of public law. IOANNIS KTISTAKIS, FREEDOM OF RELIGION AND EUROPEAN CONVENTION OF HUMAN RIGHTS AND FREEDOMS 256 (2004).

[152] Article 12, para. 1 of the Greek Constitution states that "all Greeks shall be entitled to form non-profit-making unions and associations, in accordance with the law, which may not, however, make the exercise of this right subject to prior authorization." Greek Constitution, *supra* note 34.

[153] Greek Civil Code art. 105, *in* I. SPYRIDAKIS, ASTIKOS KODIKAS KAI EISAGOGIKOS NOMOS [CIVIL CODE AND ITS INTRODUCTORY LAW] (2003).

[154] European Convention for the Protection of Human Rights and Fundamental Freedoms of 1950 (ECHRFF), C.E.T.S. No. 005, *as amended by* Protocols No. 11 and No. 14, http://conventions.coe.int/treaty/en/treaties/html/005.htm.

[155] Geoff Gilbert, *Minority Rights Under the Council of Europe*, *in* MINORITY RIGHTS IN THE 'NEW' EUROPE 56 (Peter Cumper & Steven Wheatley eds., 1999).

[156] Copenhagen Document of 1990, *supra* note 1, para. 32.6.

recognized only a Muslim minority and not a Turkish one and that the aims of the associations were to promote the idea that there were Turkish nationals living in Greece.

In the case of *Bekir-Ousta and Others v. Greece*, the facts involved seven applicants, who in 1995, along with other members of the Muslim minority, all Greek citizens, established the Evros Prefecture Minority Youth Association. One of its objectives was "to harness the intellectual potential of young people belonging to the minority, safeguard and promote minority traditions . . . and protect democracy, human rights and friendship especially between the Greek and Turkish peoples."[157] In 1996 the Greek courts refused to register the association. When the case reached the Supreme Court, it held that the Treaty of Lausanne recognized only a Muslim minority in Thrace and not a Turkish minority, and that the title was misleading because it gave the impression that Turkish citizens were living in Greece. The applicants applied to the ECHR claiming a violation of article 11 of the European Convention. The ECHR recognized that there was indeed state interference but concluded that the state had a legitimate aim to ensure that there would not be any disorder. As the ECHR observed, in the absence of registration of the association, its objectives did not have the opportunity to be tested. The ECHR held that even if its true motives were to promote the idea that there was an ethnic minority in Greece, that "did not amount to a threat to a democratic society" in the absence of language in the articles of the association advocating the use of violence. In addition, the Greek courts could always dissolve the association if it acted in violation of the objectives stated in the articles. Thus, the ECHR found against Greece because of its violation of article 11 of the European Convention.

In *Emin and Others v. Greece*,[158] a group of women from the area of Rodopi (Greece) established the Cultural Association of Turkish Women of the Region of Rodopi in 2001. This association aimed to create a gathering place for women from that region and to work for "social, moral and spiritual exaltation and establish bonds of sisterhood between its members." The competent court of first instance denied the application for registration on the basis that its title could mislead the public about the origin of its members. In 2003, the Court of Appeals of Thrace agreed with the decision of the lower court and held that, based on the Treaty of Lausanne, which recognizes only a Muslim minority and not a Turkish minority, the name of the association was against public policy. The ECHR stated that even though the evidence upon which the Greek courts based their decision was a matter of domestic law, it was not convinced that, based on such evidence, the association constituted a danger to the public order in Greece and again, as in the case of *Bekir-Ousta*, the association was not tested in reality due to the lack of registration. The ECHR concluded that once the association was registered, the courts had the power to dissolve it if it acted in violation of its articles. Consequently, the ECHR found against Greece and stated that the finding of a violation constituted in itself just satisfaction for the nonpecuniary damage suffered by the applicants.

Following the ECHR's decision, as elaborated above, the applicants reapplied for registration of the association at the competent court of first instance of Rodopi. In 2009, the Court rejected the application on the grounds that it was filed by a lawyer who was not a member

---

[157] Bekir-Ousta and Others v. Greece, App. No. 35151/05, Eur. Ct. H.R. (Oct. 11, 2007), http://hudoc.echr.coe.int/sites/eng/pages/search.aspx?i=001-82663 (in French).

[158] Case of Emin and Others v. Greece, App. No. 34144/05, Eur. Ct. H.R. (Mar. 27, 2008), http://hudoc.echr.coe.int/sites/eng/pages/search.aspx?i=001-85592 (in French).

of the Rodopi bar, as prescribed by the Code of Civil Procedure and the Lawyer's Code, which require that legal documents submitted to the court must be filed by a lawyer registered in the same geographic area as the court. The applicants reapplied and a hearing was schedule on January 13, 2010. The application was rejected on the same grounds as before; the Court reiterated the decisions of the Court of Appeals of Thrace in similar cases. An appeal was scheduled for September 24, 2010.[159]

Case of Tourkiki Enosi Xanthis and Others v. Greece involved the association known as Tourkiki Enosi, which was established initially in 1927 under the title House of the Turkish Youth of Xanthi with the purpose of promoting friendship and the culture of the "Turks of Western Thrace." In 1936, the association changed its name to Turkish Association of Xanthi. However, in 1983 the association was ordered to cease using the term "Turkish" on documents or signs. In 1986, the court ordered that the association be dissolved because its articles of association were against public policy and were incompatible with the Treaty of Lausanne, and because some members made misleading statements to the effect that the Muslim minority was a "strongly oppressed minority."[160]

The ECHR noted that the act to dissolve the association was radical, given the fact that the association had been operating unrestricted for fifty years and that the Greek courts had not pointed to any objective of the association that contravened public policy. The ECHR reiterated that even if its purpose proved that there was indeed an ethnic minority in Greece, that by itself would not be a threat to a democratic society. It also held that the existence of minorities in a state was a historical fact that a democracy had to accept and protect pursuant to international law. The ECHR concluded that there was a violation of article 11 of the European Convention because freedom of association involved the right of every person, including persons of ethnic minorities, to express their opinions and beliefs related to their ethnic background.

3. Execution of the ECHR's Judgments

The Committee of Ministers of the Council of Europe, which supervises execution of judgments by Member States, reported in 2010, that the Secretariat held consultations with Greek authorities on November 2–3, 2010, to discuss implementation of the above judgments. During the period of January 2008 and October 2010, thirty-two out of thirty-three applications to register associations having the word "minority" in their titles or indicating a minority origin were accepted. Notably, in decision No. 24/2012[161] the Supreme Court reversed a decision of the Appeals Court of Thrace, which had rejected the application for registration of the association South Evros Cultural and Educational Association of Western Thrace Minority. Areios Pagos reasoned that the Court of Appeals erred in its decision to deny registration based

---

[159] Council of Europe, Committee of Ministers, Supervision of the Execution of Judgments of the European Court of Human Rights: Annual Report, 2010 at 178 (Apr. 2011), http://www.coe.int/t/dghl/monitoring/ execution/Source/Publications/CM_annreport2010_en.pdf..

[160] Tourkiki Enosi Xanthis and Others v. Greece, App. No. 26698/05, Eur. Ct. H.R. (Mar. 27, 2008), http://hudoc.echr.coe.int/sites/eng/pages/search.aspx?i=001-85590 (in French).

[161] Decision No. 24/2012, Areios Pagos Δ' Civil Jurisdiction, *available at* http://www.areiospagos.gr/ (click on number and year of decision).

on a mere suspicion due to lack of clarity of the wording "minority of Western Thrace" without further definition of the word "minority", whether it is religious or national, and because of this, the association has hidden purposes which may pose a threat to public order. Such a lack of clarity is not by itself sufficient to justify a threat to the public order.[162]

Moreover, the State Legal Counsel has published the three ECHR judgments in Greek translation on its Internet site. The Ministry of Justice has forwarded the judgments in Greek to the President of the Areios Pagos, reiterating Greece's obligation to comply with the judgments pursuant to article 46 of the European Convention. The judgment of *Tourkiki Enosi and Others* has also been forwarded to the authorities of the prefectures of Xanthi Drama and Cavala where Muslim minorities reside.[163]

At the same time, a 2011 Report by the Council of Europe Committee of Ministers states that all the applications requesting that the decisions issued by courts of first instance prior to the decision of the ECHR on *Bekir-Ousta* were rejected on appeal.[164] However, Areios Pagos held a hearing in the case of *Tourkiki Enose Xanthes and Others*.[165] The Council of Ministers also noted the commitment of the Greek authorities to comply with the ECHR rulings.[166]

On March 2012, the Greek authorities provided to the Council of Ministers a copy of decision No. 353/2012 issued in February 2012 by the Supreme Court, which dismissed the appeal filed by the Association of Tourkiki Enosi Xanthes against the decision of the Court of Appeals on procedural grounds.[167] The Court of Appeals refused to revoke its previous decision to dissolve the association, in spite of the decision of the ECHR. The Supreme Court upheld the decision of the Court of Appeals based on article 758, paragraph 1 of the Code of Civil Procedure, which allows the revocation or revision of a final judgment only if there are new facts or a change of circumstances. It reasoned that the decision of the ECHR does not fall within the definition of "new facts."[168] As of May 6, 2012, Tourkiki Enosi Xanthes had not acquired legal personality.[169]

---

[162] *Id.* at 3 (translation by author).

[163] Council of Europe, Committee of Ministers, *supra* note 159, at 178.

[164] *Id.* at 86.

[165] *Id.*

[166] *Id.*

[167] Decision No. 353/2012, *cited in id.*

[168] Decision No. 353/2012 Areios Pagos at 7, http://www.areiospagos.gr/ (click on number and year of decision).

[169] Secretariat of the Committee of Ministers, Council of Europe, DH–DD(2012)554 (June 5, 2012), https://wcd.coe.int/com.instranet.InstraServlet?command=com.instranet.CmdBlobGet&InstranetImage=2126797&SecMode=1&DocId=1896896&Usage=2.

4. Education

Issues concerning the education of minorities are governed by articles 40 and 41 of the Treaty of Lausanne, the Cultural Protocol of 1968, and the Cultural Cooperation Agreement between Greece and Turkey signed in 2001.[170] Pursuant to article 40 of the latter Agreement, the Muslim minority has the right to establish, manage, and control at its own expense schools and other establishments for instruction and education, with the right to use its own language. In implementation of these three instruments, Greece has pursued its educational policy toward the Muslim minority by adopting a series of laws and regulations that confirm religious freedom and nonviolation of ethnic identity under the principle of reciprocity.

For example, Laws No. 694/1977 and 695/1977 On Minority Schools for the Muslims of Western Thrace and on Issues Related to Teachers and Special Educational Academy (*Eidike Paidagogike Academia Thessalonikes*, E.P.A.Θ.),[171] respectively, regulate issues of minority schools, which exclusively serve the needs of the minority in Western Thrace. The purpose of minority schools is the development of the physical, mental, and moral capacities of minority students. The subject of religion is taught by teachers who are experts in religion. The establishment and operation of schools for the minority is subject to reciprocity.[172] Greece has established 198 minority elementary schools where students are taught in Greek and Turkish. Certain subjects, such as Greek, history, and geography, are taught in Greek, and others, such as mathematics, physics, and religion, are taught in Turkish. The elementary schools are all private and are administered by school boards whose members are elected by local parents. In addition, two high schools, Celar Bayar in Komotini and Muzaffer in Xanthi, and two religious schools have been established.[173]

With respect to teachers in the elementary schools, a total of 436 are teaching in the minority educational program and 544 in the Greek-speaking program. All the teachers are paid by the Ministry of Education, Lifelong Learning and Religion. Textbooks for the minority program are provided by Turkey, whereas those for the Greek program are provided by Greece.[174] With regard to high schools, there are seventy Greek-speaking teachers and thirty-

---

[170] Iris Kalliopi Boussiakou, *The Educational Rights of the Muslim Minority Under Greek Law*, J. ETHNOPOLITICS & MINORITY ISSUES IN EUROPE 1/2007, http://www.ecmi.de/fileadmin/downloads/ publications/JEMIE/2007/Issue1/1-2007_Boussiakou.pdf.

[171] E.K.E.D. Part A; No. 264 (1977), *available at* http://www.et.gr/index.php?option=com_wrapper&view= wrapper&Itemid=108&lang=el (click on URL and then click on number and year of laws).

[172] L. BALTSIOTES & K. TSITSELIKIS , HE MEIONOTIKE EKPAIDEFSI TES THRAKES [EDUCATION OF THE MINORITY IN THRACE] 50 (2001).

[173] Association of Western Thrace Minority University Graduates, Minority Education in Greece: The Case of Western Thrace Turks (Oct. 1, 2008), http://www.osce.org/odihr/33832. *See also* Dimitris Christopoulos & Konstantinos Tsitselikis, *Legal Aspects of Religious and Linguistic Otherness in Greece Treatment of Minorities and Omogeneis in Greece: Relics and Challenges*, 5 HISTORY AND CULTURE OF SOUTH EASTERN EUROPE 81– 93 (2003).

[174] Association of Western Thrace Minority University Graduates, Violation of Minority Rights in Greece: The Case of Western Thrace Turks (Working Session 7, OSCE Human Dimension Sessions, 2010 Review Conference, Oct. 6, 2010), *available at* http://www.osce.org/home/71806.

seven minority program teachers. During the 2007-2008 school-year, Turkish was introduced as a second language in high schools. Other measures include adult education classes and counseling for Roma families, and civilization courses and Greek language courses offered to Muslim parents.[175]

The Muslim minority has raised the issue of inadequate training of teachers in the Thessaloniki Teachers Academy (E.P.A.Θ), which was founded in 1968 to train individuals from the Muslim minority to become teachers in minority schools. The Academy offers a two-to-three-year training course for Turkish language teachers, compared to similar academies for teachers that offer a full four-year training program.[176] The Muslim minority's objective is that E.P.A.Θ. offer a four-year program for teachers commensurate with other academies. On February 18, 2011, then Prime Minister George Papandreou promised that the status of E.P.A.Θ. would be upgraded and that it would join the Aristotle University of Thessaloniki as of September 2011.[177]

Greece adopted an affirmative action measure regarding minority students, designed to make possible the entry of minority students into universities that are state-funded in which entry is based on national exams. Since 1996, a quota of 0.5% was adopted to ensure that spots are allotted for minority students. Consequently, it became easier for minority students to enter Greek universities, since such students had to compete only amongst themselves and not with the rest of the students.[178] Based on Law No. 364/08 a quota is provided for employment of minorities in the public sector.[179] Moreover, the Greek government asserts that women and young persons of the Muslim minority participate in all programs and has adopted projects funded partly with EU funds that are designed to fight racism and xenophobia, and to ensure equal access to employment and intercultural dialogue.[180]

In Turkey the future of minority schools is uncertain because of the limited number of Greek Orthodox persons still living in Turkey and the fate of school property, when a school closes.[181] The Halki Seminary in Istanbul has remained closed since 1971. The European Commission and Greece have expressed concerns over the closure and have requested the reopening of the Seminary. Turkey alleges that the opening of Halki should be conditioned on Greece's taking a measure to increase the number of Turkish teachers in the Komotini Celal Bayar High School.[182] During a visit to Greece in 2010, Turkish Prime Minister Recep Tayyip

---

[175] Information and data provided by the Greek Government to ECRI. Comments by the Greek Government on ECRI's Fourth Report, *supra* note 69.

[176] *Id.*

[177] Papapostolou, *supra* note 140.

[178] BALTSIOTIS & TSITSELIKIS, *supra* note 172.

[179] *See* Comments of the Greek Authorities, *in* Hammarberg Report, *supra* note 6, App. In addition, ECRI noted that the quota in the public sector is a positive measure, since the minority is underrepresented in this area. However, it pointed out that no measures have been taken so far to implement the quota. ECRI Report on Greece, *supra* note 69, at 20.

[180] *Id.*

[181] Onar & Ozgunec, *supra* note 42, at 133.

[182] *Id.*

Erdogan responded to questions concerning the reopening of Halki by raising the issue of nonrecognition of elected Muftis in Thrace.[183]

5. Muftis

The legal status of Muftis as religious leaders and judges in the family and inheritance law of Muslim minorities was first established by the Treaty of Peace concluded in 1913 at the end of the Balkan Wars. The Treaty also regulated the religious rights of Muslims who stayed in Greece in the newly acquired lands of Macedonia, Ipirus, Crete, Lesbos, and Chios.[184] Pursuant to Law 2345/1920,[185] Muftis were supposed to be elected directly by the Muslim communities. A royal decree to provide detailed implementing rules was never adopted. In practice, elections of Muftis never occurred; the person chosen by the community was appointed by the government, as occurred in the case of a Mufti in Rodopi in 1920 and another one in 1935.[186]

As of 1991, pursuant to Law No. 1920/1990,[187] Muftis were appointed by the local prefect based on the selection of a person recognized by the Muslim community. Greece justified the adoption of this law on the ground that the Muftis are paid by the state and also perform judicial duties in civil matters in addition to their religious duties. In implementation of this law, Greece appointed two Muftis and one assistant Mufti in Thrace. The appointment of the Muftis divided the Muslim minority community, because part of it endorsed the authority of the two appointed Muftis whereas the rest of the minority community elected two of their own. Subsequently, the two elected Muftis were prosecuted for unlawfully assuming the functions of the Mufti and one of them was sentenced to a ten-month prison term under the pertinent article of the Greek Criminal Code.[188]

---

[183] Dimosthenis Yagcioglu, *Reciprocal Insincerity: Trends in Treatment in Minorities in Greece, Turkey*, HURRIYET DAILY NEWS (Jan. 24, 2011), http://www.hurriyetdailynews.com/default.aspx?pageid=438& n=reciprocal-insincerity-current-trends-in-the-treatment-of-minorities-in-greece-and-turkey-2011-01-22.

[184] The Treaty of Athens was ratified by Law ΔΣΙΓ' of November 4, 1913, E.K.E.D., Part A, No. 229. See also K. Tsitselikis, The Treaty of Athens of 1913 in the Procrustean Bed, A Classic Case of International Law and the Religious Freedom of Muslims in Greece, 1 NOMOKANONIKA 101 (2002).

[185] Law No. 2345/1920 on Appointing a Temporary Chief Moufti and on Mouftis for the Muslim Community in Greece and on Administration of their Properties, E.K.E.D., Part A, No. 148, July 3, 1920, *available at* http://www.et.gr/index.php?option=com_wrapper&view=wrapper&Itemid=108&lang=el (click on Law 2345/1920).

[186] Konstantinos Tsitselikis, *Personal Status of Greece's Muslim: A Legal Anachronism or an Example of Applied Multiculturalism*, INTERNATIONAL AND EUROPEAN FORUM ON MIGRATION RESEARCH, THE LEGAL TREATMENT OF ISLAMIC MINORITIES IN EUROPE AND IN THE UNITED STATES 109–32 (R. Aluffi & G. Zincone eds., 2004).

[187] E.K.E.D., Part A, No. 182 (1990), *available at* http://www.et.gr/idocs-nph/search/pdfViewerForm_html?args=5C7QrtC22wFWwnXHUzxPWXdtvSoClrL8P4476sndBGZ5MXD0LzQTL WPU9yLzB8V68knBzLCmTXKaO6fpVZ6Lx3UnKl3nP8NxdnJ5r9cmWyJWelDvWS_18kAEhATUkJb0x1LIdQ1 63nV9K--td6SIucada4V3d_K6_u7-MM_nmQy_qDHDwYKA37fYEUi4jgMe (click on URL and then click on number and year of law).

[188] Theresa Papademetriou, *Greece, in* RELIGIOUS LIBERTY: THE LEGAL FRAMEWORK IN SELECTED OSCE COUNTRIES 51, 63 (Law Library of Congress, 2000).

In the case of *Serif v. Greece*,[189] the applicant, who was convicted for unlawful usurpation of the title of Mufti, applied to the ECHR arguing that his conviction amounted to interference with his right to exercise his religion. The Greek government argued that the state's interference was prescribed by law and had a legitimate purpose, which was the preservation of order in the Muslim community. Under the requirement that the government must prove that the measure was necessary in a democratic society, Greece argued that in many countries the Muftis were appointed by the state and that the Greek authorities had to interfere to avoid tension among Muslims, between Muslims and Christians, and between Greece and Turkey. The applicant counterclaimed that Christians and Jews in Greece had the right to elect their religious leaders.[190] The ECHR asserted that the role of the authorities in such instances "is not to remove the cause of tension by eliminating pluralism, but to ensure that the competing groups tolerate each other."[191] The ECHR concluded that the conviction of the applicant was not justified in this case by a "pressing social need"; therefore, the interference with the applicant's right to enjoy and manifest his religion in worship and teaching was not "necessary in a democratic society . . . for the protection of public order" under article 9 of the European Convention.[192]

In accordance with Law 1920/1991 Muftis exercise religious duties pursuant to Sharia law and judicial duties related to marriages, divorces, alimony, guardianship, wills and intestate succession, and the endorsement of religious marriages among Muslims, and also issue legal opinions pertaining to questions involving Sharia law.[193] The decisions of Muftis are not enforceable, nor do they have res judicata effect unless the appropriate district court declares them enforceable. Districts courts must examine whether a Mufti acted within the limits of his authority and whether the decision is compatible with constitutional norms.[194] Decisions of the district court, which are written in Greek, are subject to appeal.[195] One scholar has noted that Greek judges are in no position to exercise substantial judicial review in the absence of knowledge of Sharia law.[196]

6. Sharia Law: Scope of Application

Muslim Greek citizens are subject to Sharia law. Currently, there are three Sharia courts in Thrace recognized by Law No. 1920/1990.[197] Sharia courts must decide issues in accordance

---

[189] Serif v. Greece, App. No. 38178/97, Eur. Ct. H.R. (final judgment, Mar. 14, 2000), http://hudoc.echr.coe.int/sites/eng/pages/search.aspx?i=001-58518.

[190] *Id.* para. 48.

[191] *Id.* para. 53.

[192] *Id.* para. 54.

[193] Law 1920/1991 on Muslim Religious Ministers art. 5, paras. 1 & 2, E.K.E.D., Part A, No. 11 (Feb. 4, 1991), *available at* http://www.et.gr/index.php?option=com_wrapper&view=wrapper&Itemid=108&lang=el (enter number and year of law).

[194] *Id.* art. 5, para. 3.

[195] For more details on the duties of the Mufti, *see* SYMEON SOLTARIDES, HE ISTORIA TON MOUFTIDON TES DYTIKES THRAKES [THE HISTORY OF MOUFTIS IN WESTERN THRACE] 175–97 (1997).

[196] Tsitselikis, *supra* note 186.

[197] Law 1920/1991, *supra* note 193.

with constitutional guarantees and the rights and freedoms enshrined in the European Convention on Human Rights. Ninety-nine percent of the decisions issued by Muftis are endorsed by the Greek courts, even when such decisions are manifestly incompatible with human rights.[198] In addition, the Commissioner of Human Rights of the Council of Europe, Thomas Hammarberg, urged Greece to ensure full review of the decisions of Muftis by domestic courts and to reexamine the issue of application of Sharia law upon consultation with the minority.[199]

The application of Sharia law in Greece, where it was introduced in 1914,[200] has generated a great deal of controversy and debate in legal theory and practice concerning its territorial application and whether Muslim Greek citizens have the right to choose between Sharia law and the Greek Civil Code. Under Sharia law, women's status is inferior to men and Muslim women are subject to discrimination with regard to inheritance or divorce. Consequently, the application of Sharia raises serious constitutional law questions because of its conflict with the principle of equality of the sexes and other human rights provisions enshrined in international conventions ratified by Greece.

Two schools of thought have emerged on the application of Sharia to Muslim citizens in Greece. The first, which is prevalent, espouses the opinion that Sharia law applies only to the Muslim minority in Western Thrace while Muslims living in other parts of Greece, including those in the Dodecanese, are subject to the provisions of the Civil Code in force since 1946.[201] The second asserts that Sharia applies to all Muslims in the entire territory of Greece.[202]

The question as to whether there is concurrent jurisdiction between civil courts and Sharia courts has also been disputed. An argument that was advanced by the Greek government and some academics is that based on article 42, paragraph 1 of the Treaty of Lausanne, Greece ought to take measures to settle issues of personal and family status of Muslims in accordance with the customs of such minorities. On the other hand, the Lausanne Treaty does not refer specifically to Sharia law or courts, it refers to customs in general that are of relevance to the personal status of Muslims. Other arguments made by Greek scholars against the application of Sharia law to Greek Muslim citizens are the following:

- Greece cannot bring as a justification the pertinent provision of the Treaty of Lausanne, to evade its international responsibilities arising from human rights instruments.

- It is incompatible with the principle of equality of the sexes, equality before the law, and nondiscrimination.

---

[198] TSITSELIKIS, *supra* note 134.

[199] Hammarberg Report, *supra* note 6, para. 3.

[200] Law 147/1914 art. 4, E.K.E.D., Part A, No. 25 (Jan. 2, 1914), *available at* http://www.et.gr/index. php?option=com_wrapper&view=wrapper&Itemid=108&lang=el.

[201] KTISTAKIS, *supra* note 112, at 36.

[202] *Id.* at 37.

- Its application does lead to violations of human rights, especially for women and children.

- Most European states do not apply Sharia law to their Muslim population, including France and Germany, which have a large population of Muslims.

- It violates the public order and morals as applied in Greece, for instance in cases of polygamy, which is permitted under Sharia law, or in the case of divorce, which is not endorsed by a court.

- Turkey, whose population is mostly Muslim, long ago abolished Sharia law.[203]

7. Case Law

a. Supreme Court Judgments

In 1980, the Supreme Court held that Sharia law applies generally to all Muslims irrespective of residency in Greece and that the role of a Mufti as a judge is constitutionally compatible with the notion of "a natural judge" as provided by article 8, paragraph 1 of the Constitution. The facts of the case involved two Muslims, both residents of Athens. After divorce, the ex-wife applied for alimony for herself and her child. The Supreme Court held that the Mufti of Xanthi in Western Thrace had jurisdiction over the case.[204] In a more recent decision No. 1097/2007, the Supreme Court held that Muftis have jurisdiction over Muslims in regard to marriages, alimony, guardianship, emancipation of minors, and wills and intestate succession, provided that the issues involved in the case are covered by Sharia law.

b. First Instance Courts

The three-member district court of Theva held in Decision No. 405/2000 that in certain instances, Muslim Greek citizens have the right to choose to be under the jurisdiction of civil courts rather than Sharia law.[205] In this case, a Muslim woman belonging to the minority in Thrace who was a resident of Theva (another area in central Greece) requested that the district court in Theva appoint a special guardian for her minor child until she contested the paternity of the father. The district court held that the case fell under the jurisdiction of the Mufti. However, when Sharia law impinges on the human rights of an individual, the Greek constitution and the European Convention of Human Rights prevail and Greece is obliged to provide the party concerned with a choice of jurisdiction between a Mufti and Sharia law or the Greek Civil Code and civil courts, the court said.[206] Although the judge adjudicated the matter in accordance with the law, nevertheless the decision drew some critical comments on procedural grounds, because

---

[203] *See also* Iris Boussiakou, *Religious Freedom and Minority Rights in Greece: The Case of the Muslim Minority in Western Thrace* 14–22, Paper No. 21, Hellenic Observatory Papers on Greece and Southeast Europe (2008), *available at* http://eprints.lse.ac.uk/23191/1/GreeSE_No_21.pdf.

[204] Case 1723/1980, *cited in* KTISTAKIS, *supra* note 112, at 37.

[205] *See* Decision of Court of Theves, No. 405/2000, *cited in* KTISTAKIS, *supra* note 112, at 38.

[206] *Id.*

the Greek Code of Civil Procedure does not recognize concurrent subject matter jurisdiction, but only concurrent territorial jurisdiction.[207]

8. Religious Foundations (*Vakfs*)

a. Background

Pursuant to Ottoman law, each *vakf* was a legal entity whose property was managed by an administrator or an administrative committee depending on its nature.[208] Several articles of the Treaty of Lausanne govern the legal status of *vakfs* of the Muslim minority in Greece and the Greek Orthodox minority in Turkey. Article 40 of the Treaty recognizes the right of both minorities (the Greek Orthodox minority in Turkey and the Muslim minority in Greece) to enjoy in law and in fact the same rights and guarantees as the rest of the citizens and to establish, manage, and supervise at their own expense any activities of a charitable, religious, or educational nature;[209] to use their language freely therein; and to practice their religion.[210] Under article 42, both parties are obliged to protect churches, cemeteries, and other religious establishments; to facilitate the opening of new religious and charitable foundations; and not to deny any other benefits accorded to private foundations of a similar nature.[211]

Based on Law No. 2345/1920, which was drafted for purposes of the Muslim communities in Greece prior to the Treaty of Lausanne, the administration of *vakfs* was given to the Muslim minority under the supervision of the local Mufti.[212] Law No. 1091/1980, on the management and administration of *vakfs* and their properties belonging to the Muslim minority

---

[207] *Id.* at 39.

[208] KONSTANTINOS TSITSELIKIS, A STORY OF RECIPROCITY: THE MINORITY VAKFS IN GREECE AND TURKEY 12 (2010).

[209] The case of *Fener Rum Erkek Lisesi Vafki v. Turkey* decided in 2007 is of relevance here. Fener Rum is a foundation established pursuant to the Treaty of Lausanne in order to provide educational facilities in the Greek Higher Secondary School in Fener (Istanbul). In this case, the ECHR held that Turkey violated article 1 of Protocol 1 related to property, because under Turkish legislation, as applied by its courts, Turkey deprived a religious minority—in this case the applicant foundation—of its property title and removed it from the land register. The ECHR ordered Turkey to reenter the property of the foundation in the land registry under the name of Fener Rum and ordered Turkey to pay €890,000 to the foundation if the property was not registered. *See* Press Release, Registrar, Chamber Judgment Fener Rum Erkek Lisesi Vafki v. Turkey, *available at* http://cmiskp.echr.coe.int/ tkp197/view.asp?item=2&portal=hbkm&action=html&highlight=34478/97&sessionid=67765319&skin=hudoc-pr-en. *See also* Fener Rum Patrikligi (Ecumenical Patriarchate) v. Turkey, App. No. 14340/05, Eur. Ct. H.R. (Sept. 15, 2010), http://hudoc.echr.coe.int/sites/eng/pages/search.aspx?i=001-99420 (in French), in which the Court held that the Turkish authorities violated Protocol 1 on protection of property because it deprived the Ecumenical Patriarchate of its property without compensation. *See* Press Release, Registrar, Chamber Judgments of June 15, 2010 (Concerning Hungary, Poland, Portugal, Romania, Turkey and the United Kingdom), http://www.strasbourg consortium.org/document.php?DocumentID=4965.

[210] Treaty of Lausanne art. 40.

[211] *Id.*

[212] E.K.E.D., Part A, No. 124 (1920), *available at* http://www.et.gr/index.php?option=com_wrapper&view=wrapper&Itemid=108&lang=el (click on number and year of Law).

of Western Thrace,[213] was designed to modernize the existing system of management of *vakfs* and stated clearly that its application was conditional under reciprocity. It defined *"vakfs"* as any property dedicated to an existing or future religious, philanthropic, or public benefit foundation. Property included in the *vakf* is the *vakf* itself and other movable or immovable property necessary for the operation of the *vakf* or its purposes. Each *vakf* constituted a legal entity of private law. The 1980 law was never implemented in practice, due to strong reactions from the Muslim community.[214]

b. *New Law on* Vakfs

Law 3647/2008, instituted a new regime on the management and administration of Muslim *vakfs* in Western Thrace and their properties,[215] and abolished the 1980 law; the Muslim minority opposed the new law allegedly because of a lack of consultation during the drafting process, and because their concerns over the powers vested in the appointed Mufti and authority vested in the regional secretary general were largely ignored.[216] In view of this controversy, it is not clear how the law is being implemented. Under the Law, *vakfs'* properties are divided *de facto* into three groups: (a) those in Komotini, Xanthi, and Didymotichon (all areas in Western Thrace) under a central administration; (b) those that exist in villages, which remain under the control of the local administration; and (c) those *vakfs* devoted to education. Other important highlights of the above law include the fact that it

- makes no reference to reciprocity,

- defines *"vakfs"* as legal entities of private law, and

- provides that income from *vakf* property can be dispensed for specific purposes, as enumerated by the law.[217]

c. *Taxation of* Vakfs

Pursuant to Law 3554/2007, the properties of *vakfs* are not subject to taxation.[218]

---

[213] *Id.* Part. A, No. 267 (1980), *available at* http://www.et.gr/index.php?option=com_wrapper&view=wrapper&Itemid=104&lang=el. (click on number and year of law).

[214] TSITSELIKIS, *supra* note 208, at 12.

[215] E.K.E.D., Part A, No. 37 (2008), *available at* http://www.et.gr/index.php?option=com_wrapper&view=wrapper&Itemid=104&lang=el (click on URL and on number and year of law).

[216] Association of Western Thrace Minority University Graduates, Combating Intolerance and Discrimination Against Minorities in Greece: The Case of Western Thrace Turkish Minority at 3. *See also* Eleni Velivasaki, Accommodating Religious Pluralities: The Case of Greece (paper submitted to a Conference on "Minority Politics within the Europe of Regions" (June 11, 2010), *available at* http://kv.sapientia.ro/uploads/rendezvenyek/mineureg/eloadasok/Velivasaki.pdf.

[217] Law 3647/2008, *as summarized in* TSITSELIKIS, *supra* note 208, at 15.

[218] Law 3554/2007 art. 7, para. 4, E.K.E.D., Part A, No. 80 (2007), *available at* http://www.et.gr/index.php?option=com_wrapper&view=wrapper&Itemid=108&lang=el.

C. Application of the Treaty of Lausanne

The Treaty of Lausanne became part of domestic law pursuant to the Legislative Decree of August 25, 1923.[219] Hierarchically within the Greek legal order, treaties ratified by Greece, including the Lausanne Treaty, enjoy a superior status. Greek legal scholars disagree on the exact rank of such treaties, however. Some claim that they are on an equal standing with constitutional norms but in case of conflict the Constitution takes precedence, while others have argued the opposite.[220] As stated previously, the Lausanne Treaty is the only treaty, along with the Treaty of Finland on the Arand Islands, that survived the League of Nations minority system.[221]

The Muslim minority is protected under provisions of the Treaty of Lausanne located in section III, "Protection of Minorities." The Turkish negotiators requested the element of religion to identify the population that was subject to minority protection partly due to the influence of the administrative system of religious communities, the *millet* system,[222] that existed prior to the establishment of Turkey as a modern state in 1923.[223]

Based on the absence of the word "Turkish" in the Lausanne Treaty, Greece argues that it has the right to object to the use of word "Turkish" by any associations or individuals who wish to be identified as Turkish and not Muslim. As illustrated above by the cases of *Bekir-Ousta*, *Emin and Others*, and *Tourkiki Enosi Xanthis and Others*, the ECHR has disagreed with the Greek courts' narrow interpretation of the Treaty of Lausanne and with their reasoning that such associations promote the idea that a Turkish minority exists in Greece; hence the ECHR has found against Greece in the above cases.

Section III of the Treaty of Lausanne consists of nine articles, including a general clause and eight articles that regulate issues relating to religious, educational, and linguistic rights of the minority. The general clause of article 37 provides that articles 38–44, which guarantee the enjoyment of rights of minorities, "shall be recognized as fundamental laws, and that no law, no regulation, nor official action shall conflict or interfere with these stipulations, nor shall any law, regulation, nor official action prevail over them." Thus, this general clause accords the rights granted to respective minorities as having superior legal force, that of a fundamental law of the State, having constitutional status.

Articles 38–45 prescribe the obligations of the two parties, Greece and Turkey, toward their respective minorities and the pertinent rights of minorities. Although 38–44 only deal with

---

[219] E.K.E.D. , Part A, No. 333 (Oct. 30, 1923).

[220] Psychogiopoulou, *supra* note 149, at 117.

[221] SPILIOPOULOU AKERMARK, *supra* note 55, at 120.

[222] Renee Hirschon, *'Unmixing Peoples' in the Aegean Region*, *in* CROSSING THE AEGEAN, *supra* note 9, at 8.

[223] Prior to 1923, Ottoman subjects were identified on the basis of religion. For example, Orthodox Christians were viewed as belonging to the Rum millet and were named Rum or Romios. *See* Notes on Terminology and Orthography, *id*. at xii.

Turkey's obligations, article 45 makes these obligations also applicable to Greece. The provisions can be summarized as follows:

- Article 38: Turkey and Greece must not discriminate against the inhabitants living in their territories on the grounds of birth, nationality, language, race, or religion, and must protect the life and liberty of their inhabitants; and must allow the free exercise of religion and beliefs in public or in private, provided that it is compatible with public order or morals. The respective minorities have the right of free movement and immigration, under certain conditions.

- Article 39: The minorities who are also citizens of the country where they live must enjoy the same civil and political rights as the majority, be equal before the law, and enjoy the same opportunities for employment and free use of their language in their private relations, commercial activities, and press.

- Article 40: Minorities have the right to create, manage. and control through their own means charitable, religious, and social institutions, and schools and other establishments for instruction and education, with the right to use their own language and to exercise their own religion freely therein.

- Article 41: Turkey and Greece undertake the obligation to assure that in areas where a large part of the minority lives, appropriate facilities are founded to allow instruction in their respective languages in primary education.

- Article 42: Turkey and Greece must give public funds to promote education, religion, and charity within the minorities. Both parties are also obliged to protect churches, cemeteries, and other religious establishments.

- Article 43: Minorities cannot be required to perform any act in violation of their faith or religious practices.

- Article 44: In case a dispute arises between the two parties on law or facts concerning any article of the Treaty, the dispute will be considered as an international dispute and each party may bring the matter to the Permanent Court of International Justice, which will issue a binding decision on the issue.

- Article 45: The rights conferred by articles 38–44 will be similarly conferred by Greece on the Muslim minority in her territory.

1. Legal Issues Arising From Application of the Treaty of Lausanne

   a. Territorial Scope of the Treaty

Historically, the Treaty of Lausanne has been interpreted by the Greek government as being limited in its territorial application to the Muslim minority located in Western Thrace. This official view is not in line with the Supreme Court's Decision No. 1723 issued in 1980[224] in which it reaffirmed an earlier opinion that the Lausanne provisions apply to Muslims

---

[224] Decision No. 1723/1980, *cited in* KTISTAKIS, *supra* note 112, at 107.

everywhere, with the exception of the Muslims in the Dodecanese Islands.[225] Such reasoning is based primarily on article 45 of the Lausanne Treaty whose scope extends to the Muslim minority in general with no specific reference to Western Thrace; moreover, another article that corroborates this view is the one that guarantees freedom of movement of the Muslim minority within the entire territory of Greece and not just in Thrace. An additional argument advanced to support this position is that only article 41 of the Treaty of Lausanne, regarding the establishment of public schools for the minority, has limited application to Western Thrace because of the large number of Muslims in that area.[226] Application of the Treaty of Lausanne within the entire territory of Greece except the Dodecanese seems to be supported by the legal literature as well.[227]

Consequently, based on article 29 of the Vienna Convention on the Law of Treaties, which provides that a treaty is binding upon each party in respect of the entire territory unless a different intention appears from the treaty or is otherwise established, it can be deduced that the intention of the drafters of the Lausanne Treaty was to make the Treaty applicable to the entire territory of Greece.

The Dodecanese Islands are under a special status because they were annexed to Greece by the Paris Peace Treaty of 1947.[228] Article 19, paragraph 4 provides a number of guarantees to all persons to enjoy their human rights without any distinction of race, sex, language, or religion. Such a guarantee is in line with UN standards, as the Paris Peace Treaty was concluded under the auspices of the United Nations.[229]

Therefore, there are two distinct legal regimes governing the rights of the Muslim minority in Greece: (a) the Lausanne Treaty, which applies to Muslims everywhere in Greece except those living in the Dodecanese Islands, a view in line with the Supreme Court decision stated above but opposite to the official view of Greece, which asserts that the Lausanne Treaty applies only to the Muslim minority in Western Thrace; and (b) the Treaty of Paris, which governs the rights of Muslims who live in the Dodecanese Islands, especially in Rhodos and Cos.[230]

---

[225] *Id.*

[226] *Id.*

[227] *See id. See also* Achilles Skordas, *The Minority Identity: From the System of Lausanne to the System of the Council of Europe, in* HE PROSTASIA TON MEIONOTETON [THE FRAMEWORK CONVENTION OF THE COUNCIL OF EUROPE] 169–73 (A. Bredimas & L.A. Sisilianos eds., 1997).

[228] Paris Peace Treaty, Feb. 10, 1947, 49 U.N.T.S. 1. The Treaty was ratified by Greece by Legislative Decree 423/1947, E.K.E.D., part A, No. 226 (1947), *available at* http://www.et.gr/index.php?option=com_wrapper&view=wrapper&Itemid=108&lang=el (click on number and year of law).

[229] *Id.*

[230] *See also* KTISTAKIS, *supra* note 112, at 107. *See also* Evangelia Lantza, The Muslims of the Dodecanese Islands: A Non-Officially Recognized Minority (Academic Thesis, 2011).

b. Continuing Validity of the Treaty

A further question concerns the continuing validity of the Treaty of Lausanne of 1923, in view of the fact that the parties to that Treaty have ratified subsequent treaties that deal with similar rights and obligations.

In 2005, the Supreme Court held that the Treaty of Lausanne was a *lex specialis* treaty and not trumped by another, newer treaty; that in Thrace, there are no Turks but only Muslim Greek citizens; that this historic fact and the recognition of a Muslim minority by the parties to the agreement, Greece and Turkey, establish the stance of the two countries in the domestic and international spheres; and that the Treaty of Lausanne put an end to any territorial disputes by determining the boundaries between Greece and Turkey.[231]

In examining the continuing validity of the Treaty of Lausanne, the starting point is article 30, paragraph 3 of the Vienna Convention on the Law of Treaties, which states as follows:

> When all the parties to the earlier treaty are parties also to the later treaty but the earlier treaty is not terminated or suspended in operation under article 59, the earlier treaty applies only to the extent that its provisions are compatible with those of the later treaty.[232]

Because neither Greece nor Turkey made any reservation pursuant to the article 57 of the ECHRFF and because both parties are also parties to the ECHRFF, one can argue based on article 30, paragraph 3, that the later in time treaty prevails, and that the provisions of the ECHRFF apply to everyone within the jurisdiction of the parties and not just to a particular segment of the population. One could also argue that article 27 of the International Covenant on Civil and Political Rights, which was not restricted in application by Greece only to the Muslim minority covered by the provisions of the Lausanne Treaty, prevails over the Lausanne Treaty as far as Greece is concerned.

2. The Reciprocity Clause

a. Textual Analysis

Since the Treaty of Lausanne came into effect, the term "reciprocity" has been used by both Greece and Turkey for political expediency and to justify retaliatory and other measures taken against their respective minorities, who are also their own citizens.[233] The bilateral approach, guided by a negative notion of reciprocity, has had a negative impact on both minorities.[234] A number of scholars from both sides have asserted that strict adherence to

---

[231] Areios Pagos, Decision No. 4/2005, http://www.areiospagos.gr/ (insert number and year).

[232] Vienna Convention on the Law of Treaties, May 23, 1969, entered into force Jan. 27, 1980, 1155 U.N.T.S. 331, http://untreaty.un.org/ilc/texts/instruments/english/conventions/1_1_1969.pdf.

[233] For a recent view on application of reciprocity by Greece and Turkey, *see* Yagcioglu, *supra* note 183.

reciprocity should be eliminated because its significance has been diminished under the prism of subsequent legal instruments signed and ratified by Greece and Turkey.[235]

From the legal perspective, both sides continue to claim that the term "reciprocity" is based on article 45 of the Treaty of Lausanne, which states as follows:

> The rights conferred by the provisions of the present Section on the non-Moslem minorities of Turkey will be similarly conferred by Greece on the Moslem minority in her territory.

Based on a textual analysis of the above article,[236] there is no specific reference to the term "reciprocity." Rather than the term "reciprocity," the Treaty uses the word "similarly," which in its ordinary meaning signifies that the same rights granted to the non-Muslim minorities of Turkey will also be accorded to the Muslim minority by Greece. If the drafters of the Treaty intended to grant the stated rights under the condition of reciprocity, they could have used the term "reciprocally" or a different term connoting a reciprocal arrangement.

Even at the time of drafting, it was known that reciprocity applied to foreigners and not to the citizens of one's state. This principle is imbedded in constitutions of many countries as well as in the Greek Constitution. Specifically, article 28, paragraph 1.2 of the Greek Constitution subjects the application of international law to aliens always on the condition of the reciprocity principle.[237] Moreover, reciprocity does not apply to human rights treaties.[238] In the field of human rights, obligations assumed by states are absolute and *erga omnes*; thus their application cannot be subject to reciprocity.[239] It is accepted that states cannot invoke the principle of reciprocity to escape from their human rights obligations.[240]

---

[234] In its 2012 Annual Report the United States Commission on International Religious Freedom designated Turkey as a "country of particular concern" due to government intervention into the religious affairs of non-Muslim minorities and the imposition of severe restrictions on the exercise of religious freedom by non-Muslim minorities, including the Greek, Armenian, and Syriac Orthodox Church, and the Roman Catholic Church, among others. The report states that due to the restrictions, "including policies that deny non-Muslim communities the rights to train clergy, offer religious education, and own and maintain places of worship, have led to their decline, and in some cases, their virtual disappearance." U.S. COMMISSION ON INTERNATIONAL RELIGIOUS FREEDOM, 2012 ANNUAL REPORT: TURKEY, http://www.uscirf.gov/images/2012ARChapters/turkey%202012.pdf. The dwindling number of Greek Orthodox in Istanbul is a testament to the ill treatment and difficult conditions under which the minority practices its culture and language. Greek Orthodox and other religious minorities in Turkey face a number of constraints in the exercise of their religious freedom. Renate Sommer, *Endangered Species: Religious Minorities in Turkey*, NEW EUROPE Issue 911 (Nov. 15, 2010).

[235] Alexandris, *supra* note 9, at 131.

[236] Based on article 31(1) of the Vienna Convention on the Law of Treaties, *supra* note 232, a treaty must be interpreted in good faith in accordance with the ordinary meaning of the terms used in their context and in the light of its object and purpose.

[237] Greek Constitution, *supra* note 34, art. 28, para. 1.2.

[238] Ibrahim Ozden Kaboglou & Stylianos Ioannis Koutnatzis, *The Reception Process in Greece and Turkey*, *in* A EUROPE OF RIGHTS (H. Keller and A. Stone Sweet eds., 2008).

[239] Renee Provost, International Human Rights And Humanitarian Law 152 (2002).

[240] *Id.* at 171.

The Vienna Convention on the Law of Treaties, which reflects customary international law,[241] states that human rights override any clauses of reciprocity.[242] Thus, any restrictions on human rights may be lawful as long as they emanate from international human rights treaties and not bilateral treaties.[243]

The argument that the Treaty of Lausanne does not contain the word "reciprocity" is very much in line with legal interpretations of a number of scholars from both sides. For example, a Turkish scholar states that this article is not about reciprocity but about "parallel obligations."[244] Consequently, Turkey will apply the provisions of the Treaty of Lausanne pertaining to the non-Muslim minorities and Greece will similarly apply the provisions to Muslim minorities. Such obligations by one state are not conditional on acts or omissions by the other state.[245] However, both Greece and Turkey have interpreted this article in its negative form rather than viewing it as imposing a positive obligation.[246]

In its report titled *Freedom of Religion and Other Human Rights for Non-Muslim Minorities in Turkey and for the Muslim Minority in Thrace (Eastern Greece)*, the Committee on Legal Affairs and Human Rights of the Parliamentary Assembly of the Council of Europe characterizes the invocation by Greece and Turkey of the principle of reciprocity as grounds to refuse to implement the rights guaranteed by the Treaty as "anachronistic" and threatening to "each country's national cohesion."[247]

b. European Court of Human Rights on Reciprocity

The ECHR dealt with the issue of reciprocity in three cases in *Agnidis v. Turkey* (2010),[248] *Apostolidis and Others v. Turkey* (2009),[249] and *Fokas v. Turkey* (2007).[250] In *Agnidis*

---

[241] In the Namibia advisory opinion, the International Court of Justice (ICJ) held that article 60 of the Vienna Convention contains rules of customary law. ICJ Advisory Opinion, *Legal Consequences for States of the Continued Presence of South Africa in Namibia (South-West Africa) Notwithstanding Security Council Resolution 276 (1970)* (June 21, 1971), at 16, 47, *summarized at* http://www.icj-cij.org/docket/files/53/5597.pdf.

[242] Vienna Convention, *supra* note 232, art. 60, para. 5.

[243] Tsitselikis, *supra* note 136.

[244] Baskin Oran, *Reciprocity in Turco-Greek Relations: The Case of Minorities, in* RECIPROCITY: GREEK AND TURKISH MINORITIES LAW, RELIGION AND POLITICS, *supra* note 136, at 38.

[245] *Id.*

[246] Tsitselikis, a Greek expert on minorities has commented that the Treaty of Lausanne "suffers from chronic misunderstandings, which undermine its legal credibility and applicability." Konstantinos Tsitselikis, The Minority Protection System in Greece and Turkey Based on the Treaty of Lausanne (1923): A Legal Overview (Background paper presented at Anatolia College, May 14, 2010).

[247] Council of Europe, Parliamentary Assembly, Committee on Legal Affairs and Human Rights, Rapporteur Michael Hunault, Freedom of Religion and Other Human Rights for Non-Muslim Minorities in Turkey and for the Muslim Minority in Thrace (Eastern Greece), Doc. 11860 (2009), http://assembly.coe.int/Main.asp?link=/Documents/WorkingDocs/Doc09/EDOC11860.htm.

[248] Agnidis v. Turkey, App. No. 21668/02, Eur. Ct. H.R. (May 24, 2011), http://hudoc.echr.coe.int/sites/eng/pages/search.aspx?i=001-104838 (in French).

[249] Case of Apostolide et al. v. Turkey, para. 71, App. No. 45628/99, Eur. Ct. H.R. (Mar. 27, 2007), http://hudoc.echr.coe.int/sites/eng/pages/search.aspx?i=001-87102 (in French; translation by the author, T.P.).

v. Turkey, the applicants, mother and daughter, were Turkish nationals of Greek origin living in Istanbul. Their application was based on Protocol 1, article 1 and the applicants complained that their certificate of inheritance was annulled by Turkish courts.[251] In *Apostolidis and Others v. Turkey*, the applicants were Greek nationals. One of the testators was a Greek national and the second was a Turkish national of Greek origin. In *Fokas v. Turkey*, the applicants were Greek nationals who resided in Greece. The case concerned the applicants' inability as Greek citizens to inherit their sister's real estate in Turkey on account of their nationality and under the principle of reciprocity between Greece and Turkey. They relied on articles 6(1) (the right to a fair hearing), 8 (the right to respect for private and family life), 13 (the right to an effective remedy), and 14 (prohibiting discrimination) of the ECHRFF, as well as article 1 of Protocol 1 (concerning the protection of property). The ECHR held that the certificate of inheritance was annulled on the basis of a law that had been abolished and, thus, was not applicable. Based on this, the ECHR held that Turkey's interference was not in conformity with the principle of loyalty and therefore violated article 1 of Protocol 1.[252]

The main legal issue in the three cases was the annulment by the Turkish courts of the certificates of inheritance of the deceased's real estate and the subsequent transfer of the property to the Turkish Treasury. Due to the annulment, Greek citizens were prevented from inheriting real estate in Turkey. The applicants resorted to the ECHR and complained that the annulment of certificates violated their right to property, as provided for in article 1 of Protocol 1 of the ECHRFF.[253]

The ECHR observed that the Turkish courts/authorities annulled the certificates based on reciprocity; hence, they claimed that Greek nationals could inherit real estate in Turkey only under the condition that Turkish nationals could also acquire property in Greece based on the reciprocity clause. Thus, the Turkish authorities justified the annulment and subsequent denial of inheritance because, pursuant to Greek legislation, non-EU nationals, including Turks, cannot purchase land in border areas in Greece unless they have permission from the Greek authorities. The ECHR dismissed this argument and noted that in the *Apostolidis* case, the affected individuals had property in Turkey, while in the *Agnidis* case the ECHR stated that the annulment of the certificate violated the right of the applicants to have their property respected.[254]

---

[250] Fokas v. Turkey, App. No. 31206/02, Eur. Ct. H.R. (Dec. 29, 2009), http://hudoc.echr.coe.int/sites/eng/pages/search.aspx?i=001-94458.

[251] Press Release, Registrar of the Court, Chamber Judgments Concerning Finland, Portugal Romania, Russia and Turkey (Feb. 23, 2010), *available at* http://cmiskp.echr.coe.int/tkp197/view.asp?action=html&documentId=863358&portal=hbkm&source=externalbydocnumber&table=F69A27FD8FB86142BF01C1166DEA398649.

[252] *See* Summary of the cases in REFLETS: Brief Information on Legal Developments of Community Interest No. 2 (2010), *available at* http://www.aca-europe.eu/en/reflets/pdf/Reflets%202010%20No%202.pdf.

[253] *Id.*

[254] *Id.*

In examining the reciprocity issue raised by Turkey, the ECHR stated the following:

> The Court reminds [the reader] that the Convention, contrary to classical international treaties, transcends the frame of simple reciprocity between the contracting parties and creates objective requirements with a collective guarantee that go beyond bilateral synallagmatic commitments.

The ECHR held that in concluding the Convention, the State parties wished not to confer mutual rights and obligations on each other conducive to the pursuit of their respective national interests, but to "create community-based public policy for the free democracies of Europe in order to protect their shared heritage of political traditions, ideals, freedom and the rule of law."[255]

Therefore, the ECHR continued, the task before it was to examine whether the effects of reciprocity violated the Convention and not to assess the legality of the Turkish legislation with respect to the European Convention of Human Rights. The ECHR noted that the prohibition against non-Greeks acquiring property in border areas applied only to transactions between living individuals and did not extend to cases of acquisition of property by inheritance. In examining the evidence, the ECHR noted that Turkish nationals had acquired property in Greece by inheritance. The ECHR concluded that the Turkish authorities' actions did not meet the test of legality and were in violation of article 1 of Protocol 1 of the European Convention.[256]

IV. Greece's Legal Obligations Toward Minorities Based on International and Regional Human Rights Instruments

This section of the report reviews the applicable legal standards arising from international and regional human rights instruments that have been ratified by Greece and thus are binding. It first reviews instruments under the auspices of the United Nations, then the Council of Europe, the EU, and finally the OSCE.

A. United Nations System

In reviewing Greece's obligations toward minorities, the starting point is the UN Charter. Even though the Charter makes no reference to the rights of minorities *per se*, three articles of the Charter are relevant to the discussion at hand. Article 1, paragraph 3; article 13, paragraph 1(b); and article 55 prohibit any distinction based on race, language, or religion in the realization of human rights. Moreover, under article 103 of the Charter, this rule prevails over other international obligations of states.[257]

---

[255] Case of Apostolide et al. v. Turkey, *supra* note 249. *See also* REFLETS, *supra* note 252.

[256] Case of Apostolide et al. v. Turkey, *supra* note 249.

[257] Charter of the United Nations (1945), http://www.un.org/en/documents/charter/intro.shtml.

1. International Covenant on Civil and Political Rights

Greece ratified the ICCPR and its two Optional Protocols in 1997 by Law 2462/1997.[258] In applying these provisions, Greek courts have declared the primacy and direct applicability of the ICCPR over national law, and this includes the Convention's prohibition of any distinction based on race, language, or religion in the realization of human rights. The courts are also bound to ensure that national law is interpreted in harmony with pertinent domestic constitutional provisions.[259]

Article 27 of the ICCPR[260] contains the fundamental provision on minorities, stating as follows:

> In those States in which ethnic, religious or linguistic minorities exist, persons belonging to such minorities shall not be denied the right in community with other members of their group, to enjoy their own culture, to profess and practice their own religion, or to use their own language.[261]

Three groups of minorities—ethnic, religious, and linguistic—are granted additional rights to enjoy their culture, religion, and language. The objective of article 27 is to prevent forced assimilation and to preserve the special characteristics that define a minority group.[262] Although individuals have a choice of whether to assimilate with the majority, as a group a minority is entitled to retain its distinct identity and culture.

From the legal point of view, nondiscrimination rights and minority rights are two distinct concepts. The right not to be subject to discrimination is linked with minority rights, but in terms of substance they are not the same rights. Article 27 provides certain rights to persons who belong to ethnic, religious, or linguistic minorities. On the other hand, article 2 of the Covenant contains the nondiscrimination principle on grounds such as sex, race, color, language, religion, political or other opinion, national or social origin, association with a national minority,

---

[258] E.K.E.D., part A, No. 25 (1997), *available at* http://www.et.gr/index.php?option=com_wrapper& view=wrapper&Itemid=108&lang=el (click on number and year of law).

[259] *See* Circular of 9/28/2000 of the Public Prosecutor of Supreme Court (Areios Pagos), *cited in* ICCPR, *supra* note 37, at 21.

[260] Other pertinent articles of the ICCPR include article 2 on the obligations of states parties to the Convention and article 26, which provides for equal protection under the law, with no discrimination on the basis of race, religion, political opinion, ethnic origin, or other status. These rights apply to all individuals within the territory or jurisdiction of a state and not just to minorities. ICCPR, *supra* note 37.

[261] *Id.* art. 27.

[262] Janusz Symonides, *The Legal Nature of Commitments Related to the Question of Minorities in* NOUVELLES FORMES DE DISCRIMINATION [NEW FORMS OF DISCRIMINATION] 221, No. 2, Publications de la Fondation Marangopoulos pour les Droits de l'Homme (FMDH) (Linos-Alexander Sicilianos ed., 1995).

birth, or other status.[263]   The Covenant contains an additional right of nondiscrimination enshrined in article 26.[264]

The Covenant's Human Rights Committee publishes its interpretation of articles of ICCPR in the form of general comments. The content of article 27 was interpreted by the Human Rights Committee in 1994 by General Comment 23, in which it stated that the right of article 27 "establishes and recognizes a right which is conferred on individuals belonging to minority groups and which is distinct from, and additional to, all the other rights which, as individuals in common with everyone else, they are already entitled to enjoy under the Covenant."[265]

Additional key language on minorities contained in General Comment 23 states as follows:

> 5.1. The terms used in article 27 indicate that the persons designed to be protected are those who belong to a group and who share in common a culture, a religion and/or a language. Those terms also indicate that the individuals designed to be protected need not be citizens of the State party. In this regard, the obligations deriving from article 2.1 are also relevant, since a State party is required under that article to ensure that the rights protected under the Covenant are available to all individuals within its territory and subject to its jurisdiction, except rights which are expressly made to apply to citizens, for example, political rights under article 25. A State party may not, therefore, restrict the rights under article 27 to its citizens alone.

> 5.2. Article 27 confers rights on persons belonging to minorities which "exist" in a State party. Given the nature and scope of the rights envisaged under that article, it is not relevant to determine the degree of permanence that the term "exist" connotes. Those rights simply are that individuals belonging to those minorities should not be denied the right, in community with members of their group, to enjoy their own culture, to practise their religion and speak their language. Just as they need not be nationals or citizens, they need not be permanent residents. Thus, migrant workers or even visitors in a State party constituting such minorities are entitled not to be denied the exercise of those rights. As any other individual in the territory of the State party, they would, also for this purpose, have the general rights, for example, to freedom of association, of assembly, and of expression. The existence of an ethnic, religious or linguistic minority in a given State party does not depend upon a decision by that State party but requires [sic] to be established by objective criteria.[266]

---

[263] *See also* ECHRFF art. 14, *supra* note 154, which contains identical language.

[264] Rosalyn Higgins, *Minority Rights: Discrepancies and Divergencies Between the International Covenant and the Council of Europe System,* III THE DYNAMICS OF THE PROTECTION OF HUMAN RIGHTS IN EUROPE 199 (Rick Lawson & Matthijs de Blois eds., 1994).

[265] Office of the High Commissioner for Human Rights, General Comment No. 23: The Rights of Minorities (Art. 27), CCPR/C/21/Rev.1/Add.5 (Apr. 8, 1994), http://www.unhchr.ch/tbs/doc.nsf/(Symbol)/fb7fb12c2fb8bb21c12563ed004df111?Opendocument.

[266] *Id.* paras. 5.1, 5.2.

a. Nature of the Obligations Imposed on States

The legal literature is divided as to whether, based on article 27, states that are parties to the ICCPR are obliged to take positive measures to protect those individuals who claim to belong to a minority, or simply to abstain from discriminating against and setting obstacles to deny such groups the right to enjoy their culture and profess their own religion. A restrictive interpretation is adopted by those who argue that article 27 is written in a negative form, and that state parties therefore are not required to take any positive measures.[267] Others, including UN Special Rapporteur Francesco Capotorti and Patrick Thornberry, an expert in the field of minorities, affirm the opposite.[268] State practice also indicates that a number of countries follow the positive interpretation, such as Australia, Bulgaria, Canada, Germany, New Zealand, the Netherlands, and Sweden.[269]

The Human Rights Committee, whose general comments are influential and carry evidentiary authority, has concluded that for the objectives of article 27 to be attained, it is necessary for states to adopt legislative and administrative measures to safeguard the cultural, linguistic, educational, and religious aspects of their minorities.[270] On the issue of positive obligations by states, the Human Rights Committee has clarified the scope of the obligations for the contracting states by stating that,

> [a]lthough Article 27 is expressed in negative terms, that article nevertheless, does recognize the existence of a "right" and requires that it shall not be denied. Consequently, a State party is under an obligation to ensure that the existence and the exercise of this right are protected against their denial or violation. Positive measures of protection, are, therefore, required not only against the acts of the State party itself—but also against the acts of other persons within the State party.[271]

The Committee noted that positive measures may also be necessary to protect the identity of a minority and the rights of individual members to enjoy and develop their culture and language and to be able to practice their religion.[272] It concluded that article 27 relates to rights whose implementation obligates states to ensure the "survival and continued development of the cultural, religious and social identity of the minorities concerned, thus enriching the fabric of society as a whole." All the contracting states, including Greece, must report on the legislative and administrative measures taken to implement article 27.[273]

---

[267] SPILIOPOULOU AKERMARK, *supra* note 55, at 128.

[268] PATRICK THORNBERRY, INTERNATIONAL LAW AND THE RIGHTS OF MINORITIES (1991), *cited in id.* at 129.

[269] *Id.*

[270] OHCHR, General Comment No. 23, *supra* note 265, para. 6.1.

[271] *Id.*

[272] *Id.* para. 6.2.

[273] *Id.* para. 9. Thornberry takes the position that the "positive view expressed by the Special Rapporteur is the correct one." He subsequently opines that positive action entails two consequences: a) a state should not interfere with actions of the minority to safeguard and promote its culture, religion and language; even states which do not espouse the positive view still agree with this principle; and b) for the interest of achieving equality between

b. *Interpretation of the Phrase 'In Those States in Which Ethnic, Religious or Linguistic Minorities Exist'*

The UN Special Rapporteur Francesco Capotorti, in his *Study on the Rights of Persons Belonging to Ethnic, Religious and Linguistic Minorities*, made the following important points:

(a) An official recognition of a minority is not a condition for the applicability of article 27.[274]

(b) If the existence of a minority group within a state is objectively demonstrated, nonrecognition of the minority does not release a state from its obligation to comply with article 27.[275]

(c) No distinction between new and old minorities should be made. If minorities exist in a state, then article 27 is applicable, regardless of the time the minority in question was created.[276]

c. *Reservations to Article 27*

A number of States have made reservations to article 27. For example, France made an often-cited reservation to article 27 that states: "[I]n the light of article 2 of the Constitution of the French Republic, the French Government declares that article 27 is not applicable as far as the Republic is concerned."[277] Greece ratified the Covenant on May 5, 1997,[278] without a reservation to article 27; thus this article is fully applicable to Greece.[279] On the other hand, the Republic of Turkey reserved the right to interpret and apply the provisions of article 27 in accordance with the related provisions and rules of the Constitution of the Republic of Turkey and the Treaty of Lausanne and its appendices.[280]

---

majority and minority, a state is obliged to take such measures that are necessary for the minority to preserve its values. THORNBERRY, *supra* note 268, at 185.

[274] CAPOTORTI, *supra* note 1, at 35. Capotorti stated, "it is inadmissible that only States with obligations under article 27 should be those which officially recognize the existence of a minority in their territory. . . . If that were the case, a State would only have to withhold official recognition of a minority to deprive it of the benefits guaranteed by this rule. The existence of a minority must be established on the basis of objective criteria." *Id.*

[275] *Id.* at 97.

[276] *Id.*

[277] Liann Thio, Managing Babel: The International Legal Protection of Minorities in the Twentieth Century 242 (2005).

[278] ICCPR, *supra* note 37.

[279] Greece remarked at the time of drafting, however, that the provisions of article 27 "should not be applied in such a manner as to encourage the creation of new minorities or to obstruct the process of voluntary integration." *Cited in* THORNBERRY, *supra* note 268, at 203.

[280] ICCPR, *supra* note 37, ch. IV ("Human Rights").

d. Implementation of the ICCPR

Implementation of the ICCPR at the international level is assigned to the Human Rights Committee. The ICCPR also maintains a reporting system to which Greece has submitted reports on its implementation of the Covenant.

2. International Covenant on Economic, Social, and Cultural Rights

Article 2, paragraph 2 of the International Covenant on Economic, Social and Cultural Rights (ICESCR) states that "the State Parties to the Present Covenant undertake to guarantee that the rights enunciated in the present Covenant will be exercised without discrimination of any kind as to race, colour, sex, language, religion, political or other opinion, national or social origin, property, birth or other status."[281] Greece ratified the ICESCR on May 16, 1985.[282]

3. International Convention on the Elimination of All Forms of Racial Discrimination

Article 1 of the International Convention on the Elimination of All Forms of Racial Discrimination (CERD),[283] which was ratified by Greece on June 18, 1970,[284] defines discrimination as

> any distinction, exclusion, restriction or preference based on race, color, descent, or national or ethnic origin which has the purpose or effect of nullifying or impairing the recognition, enjoyment or exercise, on equal footing, of human rights and fundamental freedoms in the political, economic, social, cultural or any other field of public life.[285]

4. Convention on the Rights of the Child

Article 30 of the Convention on the Rights of the Child contains language akin to article 27 of the ICCPR, providing that a child belonging to a minority is not to "be denied the right, in community with other members of his or her group, to enjoy his or her own culture, to profess

---

[281] International Covenant on Economic, Social and Cultural Rights (ICESCR) art. 2, para. 2, entered into force Jan. 3, 1976, 993 U.N.T.S. 3, http://www2.ohchr.org/english/law/cescr.htm.

[282] Ratifications (ICESCR), UN Treaty Collection, http://treaties.un.org/Pages/ViewDetails. aspx?src=TREATY&mtdsg_no=IV-3&chapter=4&lang=en (as of Oct. 1, 2012).

[283] International Convention on the Elimination of All Forms of Racial Discrimination (CERD), Mar. 7, 1966, 660 U.N.T.S. 195, http://treaties.un.org/doc/publication/UNTS/Volume%20660/v660.pdf..

[284] Ratifications (CERD), UN Treaty Collection, http://treaties.un.org/Pages/ViewDetails. aspx?src=TREATY&mtdsg_no=IV-2&chapter=4&lang=en (as of Oct. 1, 2012).

[285] CERD, *supra* note 283.

and practice his or her own religion or to use his or her own language."[286]   Greece ratified the Convention on May 11, 1993.[287]

>   5. Declaration on the Rights of Persons Belonging to National or Ethnic, Religious and Linguistic Minorities

The UN General Assembly's Declaration on the Rights of Persons Belonging to National or Ethnic, Religious and Linguistic Minorities, which was adopted by consensus in 1992,[288] was inspired by the provisions of article 27 of the ICCPR and elaborates and expands upon its principles. The Declaration supports the view that the obligations of article 27 are active and that states therefore must take positive measures, as discussed above. In general, declarations drafted by the UN General Assembly are not binding on states. However, the significance of this Declaration lies in its adoption by consensus and, hence, it reflects not only the political will of UN Members to protect the existence of minorities and their rights within their borders, but also the existing applicable standards pertaining to minorities.[289]

In its preamble the Declaration reaffirms the notion that by promoting and protecting the rights of persons belonging to national, ethnic, religious, or linguistic minorities, states will reap the benefits of greater political and social stability within their borders.[290]

The general obligations of states vis-à-vis their minorities are included in article 1. Moreover, states have specific duties with respect to minorities. The most significant duties are contained in article 4. Article 4(2) says that states

>   shall take measures to create favorable conditions to enable persons belonging to minorities to express their characteristics and to develop their culture, language, religion, traditions and customs except where specific practices are in violation of national law and contrary to international standards.[291]

Article 4(3) provides that states should take appropriate measures so that persons belonging to minorities have adequate opportunities to learn or have instruction in their mother tongue, and article 4(4) provides that in the field of education, states should, where appropriate, encourage knowledge of their history, traditions, language, and culture.[292]   Consequently, individuals belonging to minorities have the right to (a) use their language in public and in private; (b) learn their mother tongue; (c) establish and maintain their own educational, cultural, and religious institutions, organizations, or associations; (d) confess and practice their religion,

---

[286] Convention on the Rights of the Child, *supra* note 60, art. 30.

[287] Ratifications (Convention on the Rights of the Child), UN TREATY COLLECTION, http://treaties.un.org/Pages/ViewDetails.aspx?src=TREATY&mtdsg_no=IV-11&chapter=4&lang=en (as of Oct. 1, 2012).

[288] G.A. Res. 47/135, *supra* note 60.

[289] Symonides, *supra* note 262.

[290] G.A. Res. 47/135, *supra* note 60, Preamble.

[291] *Id.* art. 4, para. 2.

[292] *Id.* art. 4, paras. 3 and 4.

as well as acquire, possess, and use religious materials and engage in religious educational activities in their own language; (e) freely establish and maintain contact among themselves in their country and with citizens of other states with whom they share a common national or ethnic origin, cultural heritage, or religious belief.[293]

A 2009 resolution adopted by the UN General Assembly, on Effective Promotion of the Declaration on the Rights of Persons Belonging to National or Ethnic, Religious and Linguistic Minorities,[294] urged Members

- to ensure that minorities may exercise all human rights and fundamental freedoms with full equality before the law and without any discrimination, and

- to take all necessary legislative or administrative measures to implement the rights of minorities.

6. Commission on Human Rights Resolution 2003/54 on the Elimination of All Forms of Religious Intolerance

The Human Rights Commission's Resolution 2003/54 on the Elimination of All Forms of Religious Intolerance urged states to allow freedom of thought, conscience, religion, or belief; to fight hatred, intolerance, and acts of violence, intimidation, or coercion due to intolerance based on religion or belief, especially against religious minorities; to recognize the right of all persons to worship or assemble in connection with a religion or belief and to establish and maintain places for these purposes; and to use education as a tool to promote and encourage understanding, tolerance, and respect on religion or belief issues.[295]

Additional pertinent instruments include the Convention on the Elimination of All Forms of Discrimination Against Women,[296] and the Declaration on the Elimination of All Forms of Intolerance and of Discrimination Based on Religion or Belief.[297]

B. Council of Europe

Under the auspices of the Council of Europe, the ECHRFF, ratified by Greece with no reservations,[298] holds a preeminent status due to its broad category of civil and political rights

---

[293] *Id.* arts. 1–6.

[294] G.A. Res. 63/174, U.N. Doc. A/RES/63/174 (Mar. 20, 2009), *available at* http://www.unhcr.org/refworld/docid/49ef149f2.html.

[295] UN High Commission on Human Rights, Commission on Human Rights Resolution 2003/54: Elimination of All Forms of Religious Intolerance, U.N. Doc. E/CN.4/RES/2003/54 (Apr. 24, 2003), http://www.unhcr.org/refworld/publisher,UNCHR,,,43f313410,0 html.

[296] Convention on the Elimination of all Forms of Discrimination Against Women, 1249 U.N.T.S. 13 (1979), http://www.un.org/womenwatch/daw/cedaw/text/econvention htm.

[297] G.A. Res. 36/55, U.N. Doc. A/RES/36/55 (Nov. 25, 1981), http://www.un.org/documents/ga/res/36/a36r055.htm.

and its effective mechanisms to ensure implementation of its provisions. Although the Convention does not refer specifically to minorities, all the rights and freedoms—which Greece must ensure to all people within its jurisdiction—apply to all, including minorities. The substantive rights of the European Convention interconnect with the general antidiscrimination clause of article 14, which prohibits any distinction on the grounds of sex, race, color, language, religion, belief, or association with a national minority. Hence, members of minorities have instituted legal proceedings before the ECHR. Greece, as a contracting state, is granted a certain margin of appreciation that allows it to assess whether and to what extent it may be necessary to interfere with the enjoyment of human rights for specific reasons. Greece's margin of appreciation is not unlimited and is subject to supervision by the ECHR. Greece is bound to abide by every final decision of the ECHR. The Committee of Ministers is responsible for ensuring implementation and execution of ECHR judgments.[299]

1. European Social Charter[300]

The European Social Charter is a treaty concluded under the auspices of the Council of Europe on social and economic human rights. The European Committee on Social Rights is tasked with ruling on the conformity of state actions with the Charter. Greece ratified the European Social Charter on June 6, 1984, and accepted sixty-seven of the Charter's seventy-two paragraphs. It signed the Revised European Social Charter in 1996 but has not yet ratified it.[301] A ratification bill is pending, however. While the bill accepts many of the Revised Charter's provisions, it does not accept, *inter alia*, article 19, paragraph 12, which ensures the right of children of migrant workers to instruction in their mother tongue, and article 31, which guarantees the right to housing. The Greek National Commission on Human Rights in its review of the bill in 2010 recommended that Greece ratify article 19, paragraph 2 and article 31 to protect the most vulnerable groups.[302] The Commission opined that implementation of both articles does not necessarily entail an increase in cost and cited as examples the role of nongovernmental organizations and volunteers to assist in language teaching, and the prohibition of eviction during winter months.[303]

---

[298] Initially, a reservation was inserted regarding education of children that was later withdrawn. İbrahim Özden Kaboğlu & Stylianos-Ioannis G. Koutnatzis, *The Reception Process in Greece and Turkey, in* A EUROPE OF RIGHTS: THE IMPACT OF THE ECHR ON NATIONAL LEGAL SYSTEMS 451, 454 (Helen Keller & Alec Stone Sweet eds., 2008).

[299] ECHRFF, *supra* note 154, art. 46, para. 2.

[300] European Social Charter (revised) 1996 (ETS No. 158) of the Council of Europe, http://www.conventions.coe.int/Treaty/EN/Treaties/Html/163_htm.

[301] *Greece and the European Social Charter*, COUNCIL OF EUROPE, http://www.coe.int/t/dghl/monitoring/socialcharter/CountryFactsheets/Greece_en.asp (last visited Oct. 1, 2012).

[302] NATIONAL COMMISSION OF HUMAN RIGHTS ANNUAL REPORT 2010 at 45 (Athens, 2011), http://www.nchr.gr/media/ektheseis_eeda/107_11-EEDA_ENGL.pdf.

[303] *Id.* at 47–48.

2. Resolution 1704/2010 of the Parliamentary Assembly

The Parliamentary Assembly of the Council of Europe adopted Resolution No. 1704/2010 on Freedom of Religions and Other Human Rights for Non-Muslims Minorities in Turkey and for the Muslim Minority in Thrace (Eastern Greece).[304]

The Parliamentary Assembly called on Greece and Turkey to treat all their citizens equally without discrimination, to implement the general principles applying to minorities as evolved from the case law of the ECHR, and to respect the freedom of "ethnic self-identification."[305] The Parliamentary Assembly urged Greece to fully implement Law 3647/2008 on *vakfs* (foundations of the Muslim minority), provide appropriate support to minority schools including updating school books, permit Muslims to choose their own Muftis as religious leaders with no judicial powers, and consequently to end the application of Sharia law. The most notable recommendations for Turkey that are of particular relevance to the Greek Orthodox minority include (a) recognition of legal personality of the Ecumenical Patriarchate and the right to carry the adjective "Ecumenical"; (b) reopening of the Greek Orthodox Theological College, otherwise known as Halki Seminary; (c) implementation of Resolution No. 1625/2008 of the Parliamentary Assembly of the Council of Europe on Gökçeada (Imbros) and Bozcaada (Tenedos): Preserving the Bicultural Character of the Two Turkish Islands as a Model for Co-operation Between Turkey and Greece in the Interest of the People Concerned; and (d) resolution of the issue of registration of places of worship.[306]

3. General Policy Recommendation No. 7

The European Commission Against Racism and Xenophobia in its General Policy Recommendation No. 7 requires all Council of Europe Member States to ban discrimination on the grounds of race, color, language, religion, nationality, or national or ethnic origin. Law No. 3304/2005 does not cover discrimination based on color, language, or nationality; moreover, the prohibition against discrimination based on religious or other beliefs does not apply to areas of social protection, education, or access to goods and services.[307]

4. Unratified Legal Instruments of the Council of Europe

The following legal instruments of the Council of Europe concerning the treatment of minorities have not been ratified by Greece:

---

[304] Council of Europe, Parliamentary Assembly, Resolution No. 1704/2010, Freedom of Religion and Other Human Rights for Non-Muslim Minorities in Turkey and for the Muslim Minority in Thrace (Eastern Greece), http://assembly.coe.int/Mainf.asp?link=/Documents/AdoptedText/ta10/ERES1704.htm.

[305] *Id.* paras. 9–10.

[306] *Id.* paras. 18 (Greece), 19 (Turkey).

[307] For additional evaluation of Law No. 3304/2005, *see* ECRI Report on Greece, *supra* note 69, at 14. *See also* National Commission for Human Rights, Comments on Law 3304/2005 (2010), http://www.nchr.gr/media/keimena_agglika/2009Law_3304eng.doc.

- Protocol 12 to the ECHRFF, article 1, prohibits any discrimination against the enjoyment of rights based, *inter alia*, "on association with a national minority."[308] Greece has signed the Protocol but has pointed out the limited number of ratifications and the potential impact of the ECHR's workload as reasons for not yet ratifying Protocol 12.[309]

- European Framework Convention on the Protection of National Minorities. Greece has signed this Convention.[310]

- European Charter for Regional or Minority Languages.[311]

C. EU Treaties and Secondary Legislation

The Treaty on European Union (TEU), as amended by the Lisbon Treaty, requires EU institutions and its twenty-seven Members to respect fundamental rights, including the "rights of persons belonging to minorities" as provided in article 2.[312] This pronouncement of article 2, even though it is general in nature, elevates the rights of persons belonging to minorities as one of the "values" on which the EU is built upon. Article 7 of the TEU provides for loss of voting rights in the Council when it is determined that an EU Member has committed "a serious and persistent breach of the values referred to in article 2."[313]

As the Treaty on the Functioning of the EU mandates, in adopting new legislation and in implementing its policies and actions, the EU is bound to apply the general nondiscrimination principle based on several grounds, including racial or ethnic origin, religion, or belief. In addition, the EU and its Member States are required to combat social exclusion and to cooperate in promoting social cohesion.[314] To achieve this objective, the EU adopted two related directives in 2000: Directive 2000/43/EC, which prohibits discrimination on the ground of ethnic origin in employment, social protection, education, and access to goods and services, including housing;[315] and Council Directive 2000/78, on Establishing a General Framework for

---

[308] Protocol No. 12 to the ECHRFF (2000), http://conventions.coe.int/Treaty/en/Treaties/Html/177.htm.

[309] *See* Comments by the Greek Government, ECRI Report on Greece, *supra* note 69, at 57.

[310] European Framework Convention for the Protection of National Minorities, *supra* note 4. Greece signed the Convention in 1997 but has not yet ratified it. A few other countries have also not ratified the Convention, including Andorra, Belgium, France, Luxembourg, Monaco, and Turkey. *See* Chart of Ratifications, COUNCIL OF EUROPE, http://conventions.coe.int/Treaty/Commun/ChercheSig.asp?NT=157&CM=&DF=&CL=ENG (as of Oct. 1, 2012).

[311] European Charter for Regional or Minority Languages, *supra* note 87.

[312] Consolidated Version of the Treaty on European Union, 2010 O.J. (C 83) 15, http://eur-lex.europa.eu/LexUriServ/LexUriServ.do?uri=OJ:C:2010:083:0013:0046:EN:PDF.

[313] *Id.* art. 7.

[314] *See* Treaty on the Functioning of the European Union arts. 10 and 19, *as amended by* the Lisbon Treaty, 2010 O.J. (C 83) 47, http://eur-lex.europa.eu/LexUriServ/LexUriServ.do?uri=OJ:C:2010:083:0047:0200:EN:PDF.

[315] Council Directive 2000/43/EC of 29 June 2000 Implementing the Principle of Equal Treatment Between Persons Irrespective of Racial or Ethnic Origin, 2000 O.J. (L 180) 22, http://eur-lex.europa.eu/LexUriServ/Lex UriServ.do?uri=OJ:L:2000:180:0022:0026:EN:PDF.

Equal Treatment in Employment and Occupation.[316] Greece transposed these directives by adopting Law No. 3304/2005, discussed below.

The EU's Charter of Fundamental Rights of the European Union is part of the *acquis communautaire* and contains the following provisions applicable to minorities:[317]

- Article 21.1 states that discrimination based on grounds such as sex, race, ethnic or social origin, genetic features, language, religion or belief, political or any other opinion or membership in a national minority, property, birth, disability, age or sexual orientation shall be prohibited; and

- Article 22 states that the EU must respect cultural, religious, and linguistic diversity.

EU institutions are bound by these articles in enacting or implementing EU legislation, whereas the EU Members are bound when implementing national law. Thus, the jurisdiction of the European Court of Justice will cover instances where the EU institutions act in direct violation of the EU Charter.

In addition, the political criteria contained in the Copenhagen Document adopted by the European Council in 1993 require new candidate countries, such as Turkey, to abide by the requirement to protect minorities within their borders, including the obligation to ratify the Council of Europe conventions. The twenty-seven EU members are also bound by the EU directives on antidiscrimination and equal treatment, which affect minorities as well, and the provisions of the EU Charter of Fundamental Rights on minorities in implementing EU legislation.

1. Transposition of EU Legislation

The adoption of Law No. 3304/2005 on the Implementation of Equal Treatment Irrespective of Ethnic or Racial Origin, Religious or Other Beliefs, Disability, Age or Sexual Orientation,[318] signed into law in 2005, is a significant step not only in terms of harmonizing domestic legislation with EU standards but also towards attaining equal treatment irrespective of race, ethnic origin, religious or other beliefs, disability, age, or sexual orientation. The Law extends to the public and private sectors and prohibits discrimination, either direct or indirect; moreover, it contains provisions against harassment. It also imposes imprisonment from six months to three years and fines on those who violate its provisions. It applies in the areas of employment, social protection, education, and access to public goods and services, including

---

[316] Council Directive 2000/78/EC of 27 November 2000 Establishing a General Framework for Equal Treatment in Employment and Occupation, 2000 O.J. (L 303) 16, http://eur-lex.europa.eu/LexUriServ/LexUriServ.do?uri=OJ:L:2000:303:0016:0022:EN:PDF.

[317] Charter of Fundamental Rights of the European Union, 2010 O.J. (C 83) 389, *available at* http://eur-lex.europa.eu/LexUriServ/LexUriServ.do?uri=OJ:C:2010:083:0389:0403:EN:PDF.

[318] Law No. 3304/2005, Application of the Principle of Equal Treatment Irrespective of Racial or Ethnic Origin, Religious or Other Convictions, Disability, Age and Sexual Orientation, E.K.E.D., Part A, No. 16 (2005), *available at* http://www.et.gr/index.php?option=com_wrapper&view=wrapper&Itemid=108&lang=el.

housing.[319]   The Greek Ombudsman handles applications by citizens alleging violations of the rights of citizens or organizations by acts or omissions of the government or public services. However, the Ombudsman has no authority to represent victims in court proceedings or to impose sanctions.[320]   The Committee on Equal Treatment, which was established by authority of Law No. 3304/2005, handles violations committed by natural or legal persons.[321]

2. New Proposal on Fighting Racism and Xenophobia

On February 22, 2011, the Minister of Justice, Transparency and Human Rights published on its website a new legislative initiative on combating certain types of racism and xenophobia through Criminal Law.[322]   The proposal is designed to harmonize the domestic legislation with EU legislation—that is, Council Framework Decision 2008/913/JHA on Combating Certain Forms and Expressions of Racism and Xenophobia by Means of Criminal Law—and also to conform with the 1966 International Convention on the Elimination of all Forms of Racial Discrimination (CERD), which Greece ratified in 1970. The Committee on the Elimination of Racial Discrimination, which is in charge of monitoring implementation of the Convention, has been urging Greece to revise its domestic Law No. 927/1979, as amended, because it has been deemed inadequate to deal with current forms of racism.[323]   The law was rarely used by courts in Greece; apparently the first conviction occurred in 2008, when the Court of Appeals of Athens sentenced the publisher of the newspaper *Free Press* and one of its former columnists to a five-month suspended sentence for publishing anti-semitic comments. In 2006, the same persons were convicted for comments inciting hatred against Roma.[324]

The new proposal, *inter alia*, punishes any public incitement to violence or xenophobia either orally, through the press, or through the Internet against any persons or group of persons defined on the basis of race, color, religion, national or ethnic background, or sexual orientation, or against things used exclusively by such persons or groups, and in a manner that threatens the public order. It also punishes commission of such acts and establishing or participating in an organization that aims to commit such acts. Whereas incitement to violence or hatred is punished by imprisonment of at least six months and up to three years and a fine ranging from €1,000 to 3,000 (approximately US$1,290–3,872), commission of such acts is punishable by at least one year and a fine of €3,000 to 10,000.[325]

---

[319] *Id.*, arts. 2, 4, 16, 19.

[320] *Id.* art. 19

[321] *Id.*

[322] Ministry of Justice, Transparency and Human Rights, Proposal for a Law on Combating Certain Forms and Expressions of Racism and Xenophobia by Criminal Law Provisions (Ministry of Justice Proposal), *available at* http://www.ministry ofjustice.gr/site/el/%CE%91%CE%A1%CE%A7%CE%99%CE%9A%CE%97.aspx (in Greek).

[323] ECRI Report on Greece, *supra* note 69, at 29.

[324] *Id.* at 13.

[325] Ministry of Justice Proposal, *supra* note 322.

The proposal, which criminalizes acts of violence and xenophobia not currently covered under the existing legislation—that is, individuals and groups defined by religion and also sexual orientation—illustrates Greece's serious efforts to harmonize its domestic legislation with EU and international standards in order to combat hatred.

D. Organization for Security and Co-operation in Europe Standards

Standards adopted by the OSCE often reflect existing international legal norms and principles; they are political commitments adopted by consensus and consequently they bind states politically, but not legally.[326]

Greece, as an OSCE participating state, has pledged to adhere to such standards.[327] In clarifying Greece's obligations arising out of OSCE standards, Max van der Stoel, OSCE High Commissioner on National Minorities, on August 23, 1999, stated as follows:

> On 28 June 1990, the then Government of Greece, led by Prime Minister Constantine Mitsotakis, together with the governments of the other states participating in the OSCE, agreed to the Document of the Copenhagen Meeting of the Conference on the Human Dimension of the OSCE. The Copenhagen Document commits governments i.a. to provide persons belonging to national minorities the right freely to express, preserve and develop (individually as well as in community with other members of their group) their ethnic, cultural, linguistic and religious identity and to maintain and develop their culture in all its aspects, to profess and practice their religion, and to establish and maintain organizations or associations.[328]

Principle VII of the Helsinki Final Act of 1975,[329] which deals with respect for human rights and fundamental freedoms, including freedom of thought, conscience, religion, or belief, states that

> [t]he participating States on whose territory national minorities exist will respect the rights of persons belonging to such minorities to equality before the law, will afford the full opportunity for the actual enjoyment of human rights and fundamental freedoms and will, in this manner, protect their legitimate interests in this sphere.[330]

---

[326] *The Human Dimension of the OSCE: An Introduction, excerpted from* OSCE HUMAN DIMENSION COMMITMENTS: THEMATIC COMPILATION vol. 1 (OSCE/ODIHR, 2d ed. 2005), http://www.osce.org/training/31238; *see also* WHEATLEY, *supra* note 62, at 59. *See also* PROTECTION OF MINORITY RIGHTS THROUGH BILATERAL TREATIES 6 (Aried Bloed & Pieter van Dijk ed., 1999).

[327] *See also* Symonides, *supra* note 262, at 207.

[328] Press Statement, OSCE, OSCE High Commissioner Issues Statement on National Minorities in Greece (Aug. 23, 1999), http://www.osce.org/hcnm/52192.

[329] Conference on Security and Co-operation in Europe Final Act (Helsinki, 1975), http://www.osce.org/mc/39501?download=true.

[330] *Id.*, Principle VII (Respect for Human Rights and Fundamental Freedoms, Including the Freedom of Thought, Conscience, Religion or Belief).

In addition, participating States on whose territory national minorities exist undertook the obligation to "recognize and respect the freedom for the individual to profess and practice, alone or in community with others, religion or belief."[331] It is important to note that Greece among other participating states undertook the obligation to respect human rights, as they are enunciated in international agreements, including the International Covenant on Civil and Political Rights.[332]

During the Helsinki Final Act process, Greece proposed that the "Participating States respect the legitimate interests of people belonging to minorities already recognized by bilateral treaties or by internal legislation."[333] This proposal was later dropped,[334] as was a proposal to define "national" minority.[335] Greece claimed that the word "national" must be included before any rights could be acknowledged for such persons.[336]

Turkey stated that it recognizes as "minorities" only groups defined in bilateral or multilateral treaties to which Turkey is a party.[337] Such reservations appear to go against the right of self-identification and the basic principle that minorities exist as a matter of fact.[338]

1. The OSCE Vienna Concluding Document

The Vienna Concluding Document of the OSCE imposed for the first time on participating states the obligation to take positive measures. In addition to the general language pertaining to nondiscrimination; adoption of legislative, judicial, or administrative measures; and application of all binding international legal instruments to ensure the protection of the rights and freedoms of minorities, the participants agreed to "create conditions for the promotion of the ethnic, cultural linguistic and religious identity of national minorities on their territory"[339] and to "respect the free exercise of persons belonging to such minorities and ensure their full equality with others."[340]

---

[331] *Id.*

[332] *Id.*, last para.

[333] SPILIOPOULOU AKERMARK, *supra* note 55, at 270.

[334] *Id.*

[335] JENNIFER JACKSON PREECE, NATIONAL MINORITIES AND THE EUROPEAN NATION-STATES SYSTEM 127 (1998).

[336] *Id.*

[337] SPILIOPOULOU AKERMARK, *supra* note 55, at 270.

[338] *Id.*

[339] Principle No. 19, Concluding Document of the Vienna Meeting 1986 of Representatives of the Participating States of the Conference on Security and Cooperation in Europe, Held on the Basis of the Helsinki Final Act Relating to the Final Act to the Conference (Vienna, 1989), *available at* http://www.fas.org/nuke/control/osce/text/VIENN89E.htm.

[340] *Id.*

2. OSCE Copenhagen Document on the Human Dimension

Part IV of the June 1990 OSCE Copenhagen Document deals with minorities and affirms respect for the rights of national minorities as "an essential factor for peace, justice, stability and democracy in the participating state."[341] Because protection of national minorities raises security concerns for states, the Copenhagen Document contains a clause that also exists in other international legal instruments on minorities, to the effect that minorities may not engage in actions that are incompatible with the UN Charter, other international law provisions, or OSCE rules, including the principle of the territorial integrity of states.[342]

The key paragraphs related to the rights of minorities state the following:

(31) Persons belonging to national minorities have the right to exercise fully and effectively their human rights and fundamental freedoms without any discrimination and in full equality before the law. The participating States will adopt, where necessary, special measures for the purpose of ensuring to persons belonging to national minorities full equality with the other citizens in the exercise and enjoyment of human rights and fundamental freedoms.

(32) To belong to a national minority is a matter of a person's individual choice and no disadvantage may arise from the exercise of such choice. Persons belonging to national minorities have the right freely to express, preserve and develop their ethnic, cultural, linguistic or religious identity and to maintain and develop their culture in all its aspects, free of any attempts at assimilation against their will.[343]

In particular, they have the right, *inter alia*, to

- use their mother language in private and in public;

- establish their own cultural, religious, and educational associations, institutions, or organizations;

- profess and practice their religion; and

- exercise their rights individually or in community with others.

Participating States "will endeavor to ensure"

- adequate opportunities for national minorities, notwithstanding the need to learn the official language of the state in which they live, for instruction in their mother tongue and if possible to use it before public authorities;

---

[341] Copenhagen Document, *supra* note 1, pt. IV, para. 30(3).

[342] *See also* article 21 of the Council of Europe Framework Convention for the Protection of National Minorities, C.E.T.S. No. 157 (1995), http://conventions.coe.int/Treaty/EN/Treaties/Html/157.htm.

[343] Copenhagen Document, *supra* note 1, pt. IV, paras. 31, 32.

- that the history and culture of minorities will be taken into account in teaching history and culture in schools;

- respect of the right of national minorities to participate in public affairs; and

- the promotion of mutual respect, understanding, cooperation and solidarity among all peoples within their territory.[344]

3. Charter of Paris for a New Europe

Along with thirty-four other participating states, Greece reaffirmed the following obligations with respect to national minorities with the adoption of the Charter of Paris for a New Europe in 1990: that the ethnic, cultural, linguistic, and religious identity of national minorities will be protected; that persons belonging to national minorities have the right to freely express, preserve, and develop that identity without any discrimination and in full equality before the law; and that rights belonging to minorities must be fully respected as part of universal human rights law.[345]

In acknowledging the contribution of national minorities to societies, participating states undertook the obligation to "improve their situation." In particular, in the interests of peace and stability, they reaffirmed their commitment to protect the ethnic, cultural, linguistic, and religious identity of national minorities and to create conditions to promote their identity. They also declared that issues pertaining to national minorities can be resolved within a democratic and political framework.[346]

4. Report of the Geneva Meeting of Experts on National Minorities

OSCE transformed the issue of minorities from a domestic or regional issue to a matter of international concern. The Geneva Report, issued in 1991, states that "issues concerning national minorities, as well as compliance with international obligations and commitments concerning the rights of persons belonging to them, are matters of legitimate international concern and consequently do not constitute exclusively an internal affair of the respective state."[347] Hence, Greece may raise questions about the Greek minority in Turkey, and vice versa, at the OSCE level without being viewed as interfering in the internal affairs of the other state.

---

[344] *Id.* para. 34.

[345] Charter of Paris for a New Europe 7 (1990), *available at* http://www.osce.org/mc/39516.

[346] *Id.*

[347] Report of the OSCE Meeting of Experts on National Minorities para. II (Geneva, 1991), http://www.osce.org/hcnm/14588. *See also* Bloed & van Dijk, *supra* note 326, at 7.

V. Roma/Sinti (*Tsigani*)

Roma, the generic term that encompasses various groups including Sinti and Horamani Roma,[348] have existed in Greece since the fourteenth century. Following the Asia Minor Catastrophe in 1922, a large number of Roma from Constantinople and Smyrna settled in Greece. Currently, the Roma population is estimated to number approximately 250,000 people.[349] Other sources provide higher estimates, up to approximately 350,000.[350] Most of the Roma in Greece were born in Greece, were granted Greek citizenship in 1979, and live in Attika, Thessaloniki, Thrace, and western Peloponnese. Policy issues affecting Roma, including the housing loan program, fall within the jurisdiction of a joint ministerial committee under the aegis of the Ministry of Interior.[351]

This section concerns Roma who do not fall within the scope of the Treaty of Lausanne and live outside the Thrace region. They are called, as stated above, a "vulnerable group."[352] In 2001, representatives of the Roma issued a statement declaring unequivocally that they form an integral part of the Greek population and denouncing any contrary expression from any source.[353] The plight of Roma and itinerant people in Greece is well-documented in several key reports issued by national authorities (the Greek Ombudsman and National Commission for Human Rights)[354] and international/regional bodies.[355] The common theme of these reports is the marginalization of the Roma people due to their dire living conditions and lack of access to water and electricity. A survey undertaken by the European Fundamental Agency in 2008 reported that the Greek Roma are in the "most disadvantaged position" in the field of education.

---

[348] Roma is a generic term which encompasses Sinti and other groups who live in all OSCE countries but mostly in Central and South-East Europe. Sinti are mainly Christians. All Roma groups share common ethnic, cultural, and linguistic ties and are considered the biggest ethnic minority in Europe. *Roma and Sinti Issues*, OSCE OFFICE FOR DEMOCRATIC INSTITUTIONS AND HUMAN RIGHTS, http://www.osce.org/odihr/roma (last visited Oct. 5, 2012). The Horamani Roma, who are mostly Muslims, live in Thrace and in suburbs of Athens in Greece and speak a dialect of Romani, which is used by Athigani or Tsigani. Tsigani has been the term used in vernacular Greek and indicates the different tribes that comprise the Roma in Greece. Today, the word Roma is preferred. *See* Alexandris, *supra* note 9.

[349] National Commission for Human Rights, Report and Recommendations of the NCHR on Issues Concerning the Situation and Rights of the Roma in Greece 6, *available at* http://www.nchr.gr/media/keimena_agglika/GNCHR_Roma_Report_2009.doc.

[350] MILTOS PAVLOU ET AL., RAXEN THEMATIC STUDY – HOUSING CONDITIONS OF ROMA AND TRAVELLERS – GREECE 5 (Mar. 2009), *available at* http://fra.europa.eu/fraWebsite/attachments/RAXEN-Roma%20Housing-Greece_en.pdf. *See also* EUROPEAN MONITORING CENTRE ON RACISM AND XENOPHOBIA (EUMC), ROMA AND TRAVELLERS IN PUBLIC EDUCATION: AN OVERVIEW OF THE SITUATION IN THE EU MEMBER STATES (May 2006), http://fra.europa.eu/fraWebsite/attachments/roma_report.pdf.

[351] D. ZIOMAS ET AL., GREECE PROMOTING THE SOCIAL INCLUSION OF ROMA: A STUDY OF NATIONAL POLICIES (2011).

[352] PAVLOU ET AL., *supra* note 350, at 26.

[353] *See* ANNUAL REPORT OF THE NATIONAL COMMISSION ON HUMAN RIGHTS 2009 at 168–69 (2010), *available at* http://www.nchr.gr/media/ektheseis_eeda/ekthessi_2009_gr.pdf (in Greek).

[354] *Id.* at 32.

[355] *See also* EUMC, *supra* note 350.

Thirty-five percent of those interviewed were illiterate, and only 4% attended school for a ten-year period.[356] The report also stated that the victimization rate, related to assaults, threats, and serious harassment, within the twelve months preceding the survey was 54% of those surveyed for Greek Roma, followed by the Czech Republic at 46%, Hungary at 34%, Romania at 19%, and Bulgaria at 12%.[357] The rate of Roma employed in Greece, either self-employed or in full- or part-time employment, was close to 34%. Sixty-three percent of Greek Roma are segregated in certain areas. As pointed out in the survey, having their own neighborhoods may indicate that the group is being discriminated against and alienated from Greek society, but it also may provide protection from exposure to discrimination.[358]

Roma women and children, as well as Roma with disabilities and single-parent households, face a higher risk of social exclusion in Greece.[359]

A. Public Policy Programs

Successive policy programs implemented by Greece, such as the Integrated Action Plan for the Social Integration of Greek Roma AP (2006–2008), aim to eliminate social disparities and promote social justice and social integration of Greek Roma through an integrated approach and coordinated cooperation between ministries and local governments.

The consensus is that such programs have failed to ameliorate the plight of the Roma due to a lack of political will within local administrations in charge of implementing the programs and the lack of a central authority to ensure enforcement at the local level.[360] Resistance from the local population due to negative stereotypes and mistrust exacerbates the Roma situation. Another factor identified is the attitude of some Roma who resist change, including permanent housing, based on their nomadic habits.[361] It remains to be seen whether Law No. 3852 adopted in 2010[362] (the Kallikratis Plan), which drastically reformed the administrative structure of the country and broadened the powers of the regional and local governments, will have any effect on implementation of programs for Roma and other groups. Under article 94, paragraph 19 of Law 3852/2010, eligibility for housing is among the responsibilities entrusted to local authorities.[363]

---

[356] European Union Agency for Fundamental Rights, *European Union Minorities and Discrimination Survey: Main Results Report* 175 (2009), http://fra.europa.eu/fraWebsite/attachments/eumidis_mainreport_conference-edition_en_.pdf.

[357] *Id.* at 8.

[358] *Id.* at 14.

[359] Commission Staff Working Document, Roma in Europe: The Implementation of European Union Instruments and Policies for Roma Inclusion – Progress Report 2008-2010, SEC (2010) 400 final, http://www.lex.unict.it/eurolabor/en/documentation/com/2010/sec(2010)-400en.pdf.

[360] PAVLOU ET AL., *supra* note 350, at 22.

[361] *Id.* at 57.

[362] E.K.E.D., Part A, No. 87 (2010), *available at* http://www.et.gr/index.php?option=com_wrapper&view=wrapper&Itemid=108&lang=el.

[363] *Id.*

In June 2009, Greece agreed to take into consideration in drafting and implementing national policies the Council of the EU's Common Basic Principles for Roma Inclusion.[364] Two of the Common Basic Principles have been incorporated in the government's policies: (1) "explicit but not exclusive targeting"; and (2) mainstream integration. Under the first principle, state policy focuses on the Roma people but not to the exclusion of others who share a similar socioeconomic status, whereas under the second principle, the main objective is the mainstreaming of Roma people in education, employment, and housing.

Roma were again deemed as among the vulnerable groups in the 2008–2010 National Action Plan for Social Integration, along with immigrants and the disabled. Their lack of access to services and goods was identified as a particular problem.

On June 23, 2010, a directive was issued to all government agencies to prepare a list of measures adopted for the "vulnerable group" of Greek *Tsigani* during the last ten years, to assist the government in its efforts to take stock of measures for Roma and to evaluate the need for further actions.[365]

B. Housing and Education

Substandard housing and lack of education have a serious socio-economic impact on the Roma population. Both issues also have legal implications and have been dealt with by domestic courts, the ECHR, and the European Committee of Social Rights, which reviews implementation of the European Social Charter. Greece has been found in violation of human rights provisions.[366] Law 3304/2005, cited above, obliges the state to avoid direct and indirect discrimination and to take positive measures to combat discrimination.

1. Housing

The Greek Constitution provides for the right to housing in article 21, paragraph 4, which states that "the acquisition of a home by the homeless or those inadequately sheltered shall constitute an object of special State care."[367] In addition, Greece's obligation to provide adequate housing is based on a number of international human rights standards. Article 11, paragraph 1 of the UN International Covenant on Economic, Social and Cultural Rights (ICESCR) expressly recognizes the right of an individual to an adequate standard of living for himself and his family, including the right to housing.[368]

---

[364] Council of the European Union, *The Ten Common Basic Principles on Roma Inclusion* (June 2010), *available at* http://www.coe.int/t/dg4/youth/Source/Resources/Documents/2011_10_Common_Basic_Principles_Roma_Inclusion.pdf.

[365] Hellenic Republic, Ministry of the Interior, Decentralization, Circular No. 34947, of June 23, 2010.

[366] HELEN O'NIONS, MINORITY RIGHTS PROTECTION IN INTERNATIONAL LAW: THE ROMA OF EUROPE 14 (2007).

[367] Greek Constitution, *supra* note 34, art. 21, para. 4.

[368] ICESCR, *supra* note 281, art. 11. Greece acceded to the ICESCR in 1985. *See* Ratifications (ICESCR), *supra* note 282.

Moreover, article 16 of the Revised Social Charter provides for the right of families to appropriate social, legal, and economic protections. Greece, as a contracting state, undertakes a variety of related measures, including social and family benefits, and the provision of family housing.[369] Under article 31, paragraph 2 of the revised European Social Charter,[370] Greece must take positive measures to prevent and reduce homelessness with the goal of eliminating it.[371] Article 31 obliges states to take such measures to the extent possible. Part V, article E prohibits discrimination on the basis of race, sex, language, religion, political, or other opinion; national extraction or social origin; health; association with a national minority; birth; or "other status."[372]

In addition, General Comment 4 of the ICESCR sets minimum requirements to ensure that housing is adequate, including security of tenure, existence of public utilities, affordability, habitability, accessibility, location, and cultural adequacy.[373]

The European Commission Against Racism and Intolerance, an independent body tasked by the Council of Europe with monitoring racism, racial discrimination, anti-semitism, xenophobia, and intolerance, issued General Policy Recommendation No. 3, on Combating Racism and Intolerance Against Roma/Gypsies, which emphasizes the need to fight discrimination and bad practices in the area of employment, housing, and education.[374]

Finally, the OSCE's Action Plan on Improving the Situation of Roma/Sinti within the OSCE Area, adopted in 2003, contains a number of housing-related recommendations calling on OSCE Participating States, including Greece, to "adopt and implement effective anti-discrimination legislation to combat racial and ethnic discrimination in all fields, including, *inter alia*, access to housing," clarify property rights, regularize the legal status of Roma and Sinti people living in circumstances of unsettled legality, and ensure that Roma housing projects do not foster ethnic and/or racial segregation.[375]

---

[369] European Social Charter (revised), *supra* note 300. The European Social Charter is a treaty prepared under the auspices of the Council of Europe on social and economic human rights. The European Committee on Social Rights is tasked with ruling on the conformity of state actions with the Charter.

[370] *Id.*

[371] *Id.* art. 31, para. 2.

[372] *Id.*, pt. V, art. E.

[373] Office of the High Commissioner for Human Rights, CESCR (1991), *General Comment 4: The Right to Adequate Housing (Art. 11 (1) of the Covenant)*, http://www.unhchr.ch/tbs/doc.nsf/0/469f4d91a9378221c12 563ed0053547e.

[374] Council of Europe, ECRI General Recommendation No. 3 on Combating Racism and Intolerance Against Roma/Gypsies (1998), http://www.coe.int/t/dghl/monitoring/ecri/activities/gpr/en/recommendation n3/Rec03en.pdf.

[375] OSCE Permanent Council, Decision No. 566: Action Plan on Improving the Situation of Roma and Sinti Within the OSCE Area, Recommendation Nos. 8 and 43–46, http://www.osce.org/odihr/17554 (scroll to Annex).

a. Implementation

It is estimated that approximately 100,000 Roma live in substandard housing.[376] Greece has adopted a housing loan program that is fully funded by the national budget. It provides for 9,000 loans of approximately €60,000 (about US$78,300) each. Up to January 2009, a total of 7,686 individuals were identified that met the criteria, and 6,151 loans have already been granted.[377]

Nevertheless, the official position viewed the housing program as a "success story" because it was state initiated and funded, and put in place for the first time,[378] but Greece also noted that implementation was problematic due to misuse of housing loans and because Roma people had to furnish certain documents to prove eligibility, but many of them lacked such papers.[379]

The settlement of itinerant people through the occupation of land is generally prohibited based on a 1983 ministerial decision, Hygienic Provision for the Organized Settlement of Itinerant People, as amended.[380] The decision allows the temporary settlement of Roma provided that they meet the requirements imposed by the decision and only until permanent housing is found.

b. Forced Evictions

Evictions of Roma do occur in Greece with no legal safeguards and no offer of alternatives. Most large-scale evictions have occurred prior to cultural events. During the Olympic Games in Greece in 2004, a significant number of Roma were reportedly evicted from land that was designated for Olympic events.[381] The Centre on Housing Rights and Evictions named Greece a Housing Rights Violator of 2006 "for persistently violating the right to adequate housing of Roma." One hundred Albanian Roma legally living in Greece were forced out of public land in the Votanikos area of Athens.[382] The same families were threatened with eviction again from private land where they had temporarily settled. Following a court order issued in November 2007, the affected Roma moved to a new location, despite efforts by the Greek

---

[376] O'NIONS, *supra* note 366, at 14.

[377] PAVLOU ET AL., *supra* note 350, at 7.

[378] *Id.* (statement of an official of the Ministry of Interior interviewed by the authors of the report).

[379] *Id.* at 58.

[380] E.K.E.D., Part B, A5/696/25.4.83, *as amended in* 2003 by Joint Ministerial Decision No. 23641/3/7/2003.

[381] *See* Notes by Center on Housing Rights and Evictions (CHRE) to the U.N. Committee on Economic, Social and Cultural Rights, *Forced Evictions of Roma Communities in Greece in Relation to the Preparation of the Olympic Games* (Apr. 2004), *available at* http://www.greekhelsinki.gr/bhr/english/articles/COHRE%20Roma_Forced%20Evictions%20and%20Olympic%20Games.doc.

[382] The government threatened 100 more families. In letters addressed to the Minister of Interior, Council of Europe Commissioner for Human Rights Thomas Hammarberg raised the issue of the evictions, urging that they be discontinued until proper accommodations were found due to devastating consequences in winter.

Ombudsman and the Greek Helsinki Monitor to avoid their eviction.[383] Sixteen Albanian Roma who were among those evicted filed an application to the ECHR claiming that they were subjected to inhuman and degrading treatment in violation of the prohibition on torture of article 3 of the ECHRFF, that their right to respect for private and family life under article 8 was also violated, and that they were subject to discrimination in violation of article 14.

In January 2012, the European Court of Human Rights declared the application of *Demir Ibishi and Others v. Greece* inadmissible because the applicants had failed to exhaust domestic remedies.[384]

c. Violation of the European Social Charter

The European Committee of Social Rights has found against Greece in two cases; one in 2003 and the second in 2009.

In *European Roma Rights Center v. Greece*,[385] the European Committee of Social Rights cited the ECHR report in *Connors v. United Kingdom* of May 2004, which stated as follows:

> The vulnerable position of gypsies as a minority means that some special consideration should be given to their needs and their different lifestyle both in the relevant regulatory planning framework and in reaching decisions in particular cases. To this extent, there is thus a positive obligation imposed on the Contracting States by virtue of Article 8 to facilitate the gypsy way of life.[386]

The European Committee found that

> Greece has failed to take sufficient measures to improve the living conditions of the Roma and that the measures taken have not yet achieved what is required by the Charter, notably by reason of the insufficient means for constraining local authorities or sanctioning them. It finds on the evidence submitted that a significant number of Roma are living in conditions that fail to meet minimum standards and therefore the situation is in breach of the obligation to promote the right of families to adequate housing laid down in Article 16.[387]

Taking into account that article 16 imposes an obligation of conduct but not necessarily of results, the Committee still found against Greece due to "excessive numbers of Roma living in sub-standard housing conditions."[388] The Committee concluded that Greece violated article 16

---

[383] PAVLOU ET AL., *supra* note 350, at 35.

[384] Demir Ibishi et al. v. Greece , Eur. Ct. H.R. (Jan. 4, 2012), http://hudoc.echr.coe.int/sites/eng/pages/search.aspx?i=001-108657 (in French).

[385] European Roma Rights Center v. Greece, Complaint No. 15/2003, Decision on the Merits (Eur. Comm. Soc. Rts., Dec. 8, 2004), http://www.coe.int/t/dghl/monitoring/socialcharter/Complaints/CC15Merits_en.pdf.

[386] *Id.* para. 20 (quoting Connors v. United Kingdom, App. No. 66746/01, para. 84, Eur. Ct. H.R. (May 27, 2004) (citations in original omitted)).

[387] *Id.* para. 42.

[388] *Id.* para. 43.

because of the insufficient number of permanent homes, the lack of temporary facilities, and forced evictions.[389]

In *International Centre for the Legal Protection of Human Rights* (INTERIGHTS) *v. Greece*,[390] INTERIGHTS claimed that Greece allegedly violated article 16 of the European Social Charter due to lack of suitable accommodations for the Roma people living in Greece. More specifically, it argued that there are close to 300,000 individuals of Roma origin in Greece, a large number of whom live in fifty-two dangerous quarters. Pursuant to the Integrated Action Plan for Roma (IAP) adopted by Greece, sixty temporary sites were to be constructed and none was completed (as of 2009). INTERIGHTS attributed the problem to the erroneous implementation of housing loans, which required that only Roma who already had a plot and were in possession of a certificate of permanent residence were eligible for loans. INTERIGHTS argued that Roma are systematically evicted, with no prior notification and no alternative accommodation.[391]

Greece argued that the IAP was revised a number of times to make some concessions and that 9,000 loans were made available for €60,000 each. It clarified that there is no requirement for permanent residence or for owning a plot. It also pointed out that the Roma were beneficiaries of the Worker's Housing Association, which also constructed a settlement for Roma.[392] With regard to forced evictions, Greece argued that the Roma are evicted from private land and that the rights of legal owners of the land trump those of the Roma.

The European Social Committee, in recalling its earlier decision in 2004 in which it found against Greece, noted the progress made in improving the living conditions of Roma but still found that, based on significant evidence, "many Roma continue to live in settlements which fail to meet minimum standards."[393] With respect to evictions, the Committee stated that illegal occupation of a place or a dwelling may be grounds for eviction; however, the eviction should take place pursuant to applicable rules of procedure, be protective of the rights of the evicted persons, and be carried out in a manner that respects the dignity of the affected Roma. The Committee found against Greece in the case of evictions, because Greece did not provide evidence that the law on evictions in Greece provides for prior consultation with those to be evicted, nor did it demonstrate that the law provides for alternative accommodations.[394]

---

[389] *Id.*, Conclusions of the Committee at 73.

[390] INTERIGHTS v. Greece, Complaint No. 49/2008, Decision on the Merits (Eur. Comm. Soc. Rts., Dec. 11, 2009), http://www.coe.int/t/dghl/monitoring/socialcharter/Complaints/CC49Merits_en.pdf.

[391] *Id.*

[392] *Id.* paras. 27–34

[393] *Id.* para. 38.

[394] *Id.* para. 62.

2. Education

The Greek educational system provides for mandatory schooling for nine years according to the Constitution's mandate.[395] Greece is also bound by article 29 of the Convention on the Rights of the Child, which calls for respect of a child's cultural identity, language, and values in the education policy of the state, and article 30, which recognizes the right of a child to enjoy his or her own culture and practice his or her own religion.[396] Greece has not made a reservation to article 30.

Greece's main efforts toward Roma children are centered on mainstreaming them into existing schools, in the same classes with other children; improving their participation in elementary and secondary education; and avoiding absenteeism from school to the extent possible. Absenteeism occurs often and to a large scale among Roma children. Two government-sponsored programs funded partly by the EU—Education of Gypsi Children and Integration of Gypsi Children into Schools—have been implemented to assist Roma children in enrolling and staying in school. The programs include remedial and preschool classes, teacher training, and other efforts, but have not had a dramatic impact.[397] The Ministry of Education, Lifelong Learning and Religion claimed that the programs were instrumental in reducing drop-out levels; however, other sources dispute such claims.[398] Since 2000 the introduction of the Roma student card has facilitated the enrollment of children who had faced difficulties in enrolling due to a lack of documents and proof of vaccinations.[399] On March 3, 2010, the Minister of Education initiated a new program, Active Inclusion of Roma Children in National Education, which is partly funded by the European Social Fund. The program is designed for schools with a large enrollment of Roma children to combat absenteeism and to facilitate their integration within the national education system. It provides for the appointment of special mediators, special training classes for teachers, and special support for children, parents, and teachers. Other features of this program include after-school activities and support classes.[400]

Despite the nonsegregation policy espoused by the State, in effect Roma children are often taught in separate classes or even in different buildings due to concerns and strong objections expressed by local parents.[401] *Sampanis and Others v. Greece*, which was decided by the ECHR on June 6, 2008, involved eleven Greek Roma living in a residential area (Psari) near

---

[395] Greek Constitution, *supra* note 34, art. 16, para. 3.

[396] Convention on the Rights of the Child, *supra* note 60, arts. 29, 30. Greece signed the Convention in January 1990 and ratified it in May 1993. *See* Ratifications (Convention on the Rights of the Child), *supra* note 287.

[397] U.N. Human Rights Council, *supra* note 18, at 20.

[398] EUMC, *supra* note 350, at 26.

[399] *Id.* at 27.

[400] See information provided to the Committee of Ministers following the Sampanis Case v. Greece. Supervision of the Execution of Judgments of the European Court of Human Rights at 194, Council of Europe, Committee of Ministers 4th Annual Report (2010), *available at* http://www.coe.int/t/dghl/monitoring/execution/Source/Publications/CM_annreport2010_en.pdf.

[401] *Id.*

Aspropyrgos who, along with other Roma, tried to enroll their children in the local school.[402] The Roma families were prompted by a 2004 announcement by the Minister of Education on the significance of integrating Roma children within the mainstream educational system, and a visit by the Secretary for the Education of Persons of Greek Origin and the Greek Helsinki Monitor, who encouraged parents to enroll their children in school. The applicants alleged that the head teachers of two schools, because of a lack of instructions from authorities, refused to enroll the children and promised to notify them once the necessary notification circular was provided. The Greek government contested the allegations and claimed, *inter alia*, that during November-December of 2004, a number of elementary school teachers visited the residential area of Roma to convince them to send their children to school. Meanwhile, local authorities decided that Roma students of the early elementary grades could be included in the already overcrowded local schools in Aspropyrgos and that remedial classes would be established to prepare older children for integration into regular classes. In June 2005, through the efforts of a human rights organization for Roma in Greece, thirty-four Roma children were enrolled for the period of 2005–2006.

At the beginning of the school year, parents of non-Roma children strongly protested because of the admission of Roma children in the same school as their children and demanded that the Roma children be transferred to another building. In October 2005, after pressure from teachers, as the applicants claimed, they signed a statement that they wished their children to be taught in a building separate from the school. Consequently, for the remainder of 2005, the children were taught in separate premises.

The applicants claimed before the ECHR that their children were subject to discriminatory treatment, without any reasonable or objective justification, based on article 14 in conjunction with article 2 of Protocol 1 of the ECHRFF regarding the right to education. The ECHR noted that the Roma children had missed an entire school year and even though the actions protested by local parents could not be attributed to the Greek government, it could be assumed that the parents' protests affected the decision of the school authorities to place the Roma children in a separate building. The ECHR also noted that even if the Roma parents had only asked for information from local school authorities, as the latter claimed, there was no doubt in the judges' mind that the parents had expressed their wish to enroll their children.

Following the *Sampanis* case, the Greek authorities advised the Council of Ministers that the preparatory classes established in 2005 were discontinued at the end of the 2007–2008 school year. The applicants' children were enrolled in a new school that follows the general criteria that Roma children should not constitute more than 50% of a class. The applicants' representative stated that the children should be enrolled in a school closer to the Roma community rather than in the newly established school. The Greek authorities also stated that parents of non-Roma children boycotted the new school and sent their children to private schools.[403]

---

[402] Sampanis and Others v. Greece, App. No. 32526/05, Eur. Ct. H.R. (June 5, 2008), http://hudoc.echr. coe.int/sites/eng/pages/search.aspx?i=001-86798 (in French).

[403] Council of Europe, Committee of Ministers, Supervision of the Execution of Judgments of the European Court of Human Rights, Annual Report 2010 at 178 (Apr. 2011), http://www.coe.int/t/dghl/monitoring/ execution/Source/Publications/CM_annreport2010_en.pdf.

VI. Freedom of Religion: Juridical Status of Religious Communities

The constitutional framework for freedom of religion is based on article 13,[404] which proclaims that the right to freedom of religion is inviolable, that every known religion shall be practiced freely, and that the exercise of worship is free as long as it does not offend the public order and morals.[405] It also prohibits proselytism in general,[406] and subjects the ministers of all known religions to the same supervision by the Greek states as that of the ministers of the Christian Orthodox religion, and requires the same obligations as those required of Christian Orthodox ministers.[407] The notion of a "known" religion has been interpreted by the Council of State and the Supreme Court to denote any religion that is public, with no secret rituals or dogmas, which does not constitute an unlawful union, or a fictitious association or organization with illegal aims, and which does not violate the public order and morals.[408] Other provisions referring to the freedom of religion include article 5(2), which provides that all individuals within Greece enjoy full protection of their life, honor, and liberty irrespective of nationality, race, language, and religious or political beliefs.[409] The Constitution requires that education, which is one of the basic missions of the Greek state, promote the development of national and religious consciousness.[410]

There is no separation of church and state in Greece; rather, both are interlinked in a *sui generis* relationship, as illustrated by the notable beginning of the Greek Constitution "in the name of the Holy and Consubstantial and Indivisible Trinity" and reinforced by article 3, which declares that the "prevailing religion in Greece is that of the Eastern Orthodox Church of Christ." This phrase has been included in all Constitutions in Greece, including the first constitutional text adopted in 1821 at the beginning of the Greek revolution against Turkish domination. The notion of a prevailing religion is not equivalent to an official or state church. It is mainly an acknowledgement that it is the religion of the majority of Greek citizens.[411]

---

[404] Greek Constitution, *supra* note 34, art. 13.

[405] Public order is a dynamic concept and has been defined by the courts as comprising the fundamental rules and principles which apply at a particular time in the country and which reflect the legal, economic, social, religious, and moral views and opinions that govern a lawful way of living. On the other hand, the test as to whether an action is in conformity with morals is that of a reasonable average man who is guided by morality and equity. GEORGIOS ANDROUTSOPOULOS, HE THRESKEYTIKE ELEUTHERIA KATA THN NOMOLOGIA TOU AREIOU PAGOU [RELIGIOUS FREEDOM IN THE SUPREME COURT] 251–53 (2010).

[406] The general prohibition against proselytizing applies to any religion, not just the Greek Orthodox religion. The prior Constitution banned proselytism only with respect to the Greek Orthodox religion and not other known religions. KTISTAKIS, *supra* note 151, at 125.

[407] Greek Constitution, *supra* note 34, art. 13.

[408] ANDROUTSOPOULOS, *supra* note 405, at 246. Several religions have been declared as known religions, including Catholicism, Jehovah's Witnesses, Evangelicals, Seventh-Day Adventists, Methodists, and Islam.

[409] *Id.*

[410] Greek Constitution, *supra* note 34, art. 16, para. 2.

[411] ANDROUTSOPOULOS, *supra* note 405, at 61.

It should be noted that the existence of a predominant religion or even a state religion is not on its own seen to be in conflict with freedom of religion, which is enshrined not only in the Greek Constitution but also in several human rights instruments that are binding on Greece.[412] The status of the Greek Orthodox Church is not in conflict with EU treaty law, because under the Lisbon Treaty, the EU is required to respect and not prejudice the status of churches, religious associations, and communities within EU Member States.[413] The close relationship of church and state in Greece is due to the influential role of the Eastern Orthodox Church in the political and economic terrain and the everyday lives of the majority of the population. Legal scholars have clarified that the "prevailing religion" term possesses a twofold meaning: (a) it acknowledges that it is the religion of the majority of the population, which is Greek Orthodox; and (b) it recognizes the Church's significant contributions to protecting Hellenism during the 400 years of Ottoman rule and its special role in the Greek War of Independence in 1821–1830.[414] In a legal opinion issued in 2005, the Supreme Court of Greece stated as follows:

> [The] constitutional pronouncement of the Orthodox Church of Christ as the prevailing religion, does not entail that the constitution grants the church a higher status over other religions. Simply, the term "prevailing" signifies the central role of Orthodoxy during the historical path of the Greek nation, especially at the time of the Turkish occupation, and renders lawful the placing of the Church under the special care of the States.[415]

The Orthodox Church is inseparably united in doctrine with the Great Church of Christ in Constantinople, is autocephalous, and is administered by the Holy Synod of serving Bishops and the Permanent Holy Synod originating thereof and assembled as required by the Statutory Charter of the Church pursuant to the provisions of the Patriarchal Tome of June 29, 1850, and the Synodal Act of September 4, 1928.[416]

Greece funds part of the Orthodox Church's budget, in lieu of payment for the Church relinquishing large pieces of land to the Greek state to provide housing for 1.9 million Greek refugees after the Asia Minor Catastrophe of 1922. Consequently, pursuant to the official position, this does not amount to preferential treatment but is based on a legally binding settlement between Greece and the Church.[417]

---

[412] European Commission for Democracy Through Law, Venice Commission on the Legal Status of Religious Communities in Turkey para. 18, http://www.venice.coe.int/docs/2010/CDL-AD(2010)005-e.asp.

[413] Treaty on the Functioning of the European Union, *supra* note 314, art. 17.

[414] Charalambos K. Papastathis, *The Hellenic Republic and the Prevailing Religion*, 816 BYU L. REV. 815 (1996); *see also* Ismini Kriaris-Catranis, *Freedom of Religion Under the Greek Constitution*, 47 REV. HEL. DR. INT. 397, 406 (1994).

[415] Legal Opinion A.P. 2/2005, *cited in* ANDROUTSOPOULOS, *supra* note 405, at 67.

[416] Law No. 690/1977 on the Charter of the Church of Greece art. 1, E.K.E.D., Part A. No. 146 (1977), *available at* http://www.et.gr/idocs-nph/search/pdfViewerForm html?args=5C7QrtC22wHit7hKgn Q3o3dtvSoClrL8NFVwjN9oWbZ5MXD0LzQTLWPU9yLzB8V68knBzLCmTXKaO6fpVZ6Lx3UnKl3nP8NxdnJ5 r9cmWyJWelDvWS_18kAEhATUkJb0x1LIdQ163nV9K--td6SIuddslq2iRTlxAqRp2nwxD4Qipmidj2yvt_YN-nPRse8p.

[417] See Comments by the Greek Government, ECRI Report on Greece, *supra* note 69, at 61.

A. Authorization to Build and Operate Places of Worship

Article 18 of the ICCPR makes a distinction between freedom of thought, conscience, religion, or belief, and freedom to manifest one's religion or belief. While no limitations are permitted on freedom of thought, conscience, or belief because such freedoms are guaranteed unconditionally, the right to manifest one's religion either individually or in community with others, publicly or in private, "may be exercised."[418] Thus, it could be argued that the permit that Greece requires for the opening of temples or places of worship does not in itself constitute a violation of the right to freedom of religion, as long it does not amount to a discriminatory practice among religions or abuse of the right of individuals or government agencies involved in the process. However, the requirement of obtaining a permit raises legal issues because its application often leads to discriminatory practices and a strict interpretation by the Greek courts. For instance, in 1976, the Council of State held that "actual need" forms a distinct, independent ground for refusing the issuance of a permit, irrespective of fulfilling the other criteria, and places one more hurdle in the process of obtaining a permit.[419]

Building a new Orthodox Church is subject to a simple permission granted by the Organization of Administration of Church Property.[420] Any other religion must obtain a permit prior to construction and operation of a house of worship. This requirement has been in force since 1938, when Law No. 1369/1938 was enacted.[421] The permission is granted by the recognized ecclesiastical authority, the Orthodox Church, and the Ministry of Education, Lifelong Learning and Religion approves the permit.[422] If the authorization is denied, the aggrieved applicants have access to the Council of State (Supreme Administrative Court) to seek a remedy.

1. Case Law: Unauthorized Places of Worship

The case of *Manoussakis and Others v. Greece*[423] illustrates the problems that non-Orthodox denominations and religions, in this case Jehovah's Witnesses, encounter. The applicants, all Jehovah's Witnesses, rented an all-purpose room in Crete, and asked the Minister of Education's permission to use it as a place of worship. Meanwhile, the local church notified the police authorities that an unauthorized place of worship was being operated. From November 1983 to December 1984, the applicants received five letters from the Minister of Education informing them that he had not made a decision due to not having received all necessary documentation from other authorities. In 1986, the public prosecutor initiated criminal proceedings against the applicants based on Law No. 1363/1938 for having established and

---

[418] Human Rights Committee, *supra* note 37, para. 4; OSCE/ODIHR Guidelines, *supra* note 37.

[419] Decision 4079/1976 of the Council of State, *cited in* Stavros, *supra* note 40, at 121.

[420] Law No. 590/1977 art. 47, para. 2, E.K.E.D.

[421] Law No. 1369/1938, on Holy Churches and Chapels, E.K.E.D., Part. A. No. 317, *available at* http://www.et.gr/index.php?option=com_wrapper&view=wrapper&Itemid=108&lang=el.

[422] Law 1363/1938 art. 1, *as amended by* Law 1672/1939 art. 1, May 20/June 2, 1939, Royal Decree, E.K.E.D., Part A., No. 317.

[423] Case of Manoussakis and Others v. Greece, App. No. 18748/91, Eur. Ct. H.R. (1996), http://hudoc.echr.coe.int/sites/eng/pages/search.aspx?i=001-58071.

operated a place of worship without the necessary authorization from the local church authorities and the Minister of Education and Religious Affairs.

When the case reached the ECHR, the government furnished a number of earlier decisions of the Supreme Administrative Court that had quashed decisions of the Minister of Education refusing authorizations on the ground that Jehovah's Witnesses engage in proselytism, or because there was an Orthodox Church in close proximity to the proposed worship site. The government also argued that the Minister of Education had the authority to grant or refuse authorization, but that authority was not unlimited. Thus, the Minister was legally obliged to grant the permission if the three conditions were met: the request was made from a known religion, there was no danger to public order or public morals, and there was no danger of proselytism. The Court observed that the Supreme Administrative Court had developed case law that placed restraints on the Minister's power and held that the local church authority had a "purely consultative role." The Court also observed, from other cases cited by the applicants, that the government was prone to use the criteria established by law "to impose rigid, or indeed prohibitive conditions on practice or religious beliefs by certain non-orthodox movements, in particular Jehovah's witnesses." The ECHR found against Greece and held that the conviction had a "direct effect on the applicant's freedom of religion" and could not be deemed proportionate to the legitimate aim pursued or necessary in a democratic society.[424]

A 2001 Supreme Court decision held that the requirement of prior authorization itself is not in conflict with the Greek Constitution and the European Convention on Human Rights, provided that a number of criteria are applied and fulfilled, including that the applicants believe and follow the rituals of a known religion,[425] that the religion does not offend public order or morals, and that practitioners will not engage in proselytism. The Court ordered that the role of the Minister of Education and Religious Affairs must be limited to reviewing the conditions contained in articles 13(2) of the Constitution and article 9(2) of the ECHR. As far as the criterion of "actual need," the Supreme Court ruled that the power of the administration to make the opening of a new place of worship conditional on the existence of a real need of the applicants violated the Constitution and the ECHR.[426]

In the case of *Tsavachidis v. Greece*,[427] the Greek government recognized that it interfered unduly with the applicant's right to operate a place of worship and came to an agreement with the applicant, who was a Jehovah's Witness and was charged with operating a place of worship without obtaining the required permission from the local church authorities and the Minister of Education and Religious Affairs, as required by law. The European Commission had concluded that, indeed, there was a violation of article 8. When the case reached the Grand

---

[424] *Id.* paras. 48, 53.

[425] Supreme Court Decision No. 20/2001 (Penal case) plenum. *See also* ANDROUTSOPOULOS, *supra* note 405, at 212. The Council of State (Highest Administrative Court) has given the status of a known religion to the following religions or dogmas: the Protestant dogma of the Free Evangelic Church, the Church of the Christian Brothers, the Seventh-Day Adventists and Jehovah's Witnesses.

[426] Decision No. 20/2001, *supra* note 425.

[427] Tsavachidis v. Greece, App. No. 28802/95, Eur. Ct. H.R., Jan. 21, 2009, *available at* http://hudoc.echr.coe.int/sites/eng/pages/search.aspx?i=001-58323.

Chamber of the ECHR, a copy of an agreement between the government of Greece and the applicant was forwarded in which the government offered a satisfactory amount of compensation and a statement confirming that Jehovah's Witnesses in Greece are not subject to secret surveillance by the government because of their religious convictions, and never will be. On January 21, 1999, the Grand Chamber found that the agreement afforded the applicant appropriate satisfaction and struck the case from its list.[428]

Law No. 3467, enacted in 2006, abolishes the requirement of permission from the local bishop.[429] It specifically states that for establishing, building, or operating a church (*naos*) or house of prayer of any creed or religion, with the exception of the Orthodox Church of Greece, the permission or opinion of the local ecclesiastical authority is no longer needed.[430] Thus, an application for the issuance of a permit to establish or operate a church or a house of prayer must be sent directly to the Ministry of Education, Lifelong Learning and Religion.

In 2009, the Greek Ombudsman stated that during 2006–2009, it received a large number of complaints reporting long delays in the issuance of permits for building or opening a house of prayer for non-Orthodox religious communities.[431] He attributed the recurring problem to a recent legal opinion issued by the Legal Council of State, which goes far beyond constitutional restraints, town and city regulations, and the parameters of decisions of the Supreme Court and the ECHR. The opinion has added the extra requirement of showing "real need to establish a house of prayer" and has established not only proselytism as an obstacle to issuing a permit but also "any other intervention against the prevailing religion."[432]

2. Disputes Involving the Old Calendarists

Old Calendarists are recognized as Greek Orthodox but are distinct from the Greek Orthodox Church because they adhere to the Julian calendar as a basis to celebrate religious holidays. They also claim to be "true Orthodox Christians."[433] They lack legal status because constitutionally only the Greek Orthodox Church is the predominant religion. In the words of a memorandum of the Holy Synod, Old Calendarists "are neither schismatics nor heterodox; and so they cannot claim the right to a parallel and independent existence as Orthodox Christians alongside the Church of Greece."[434] Old Calendarists have experienced infringement of their freedom of religion, due to delays in permits to build churches. On the other hand, being

---

[428] *Id.* paras. 24–26.

[429] Law 3467/2006, on Education and Other Provisions, art. 27, E.K.E.D., Part A. No. 128 (2006), *available at* http://www.et.gr/index.php?option=com_wrapper&view=wrapper&Itemid=108&lang=el.

[430] *Id.* For more information on the necessary permission to open a church or a house of prayer, see ANDROUTSOPOULOS, *supra* note 405, at 14.

[431] Press Release, Synigoros tou Polite (Greek Ombudsman – Independent Authority), Greek Ombudsman Intervenes for the Delay of a Permit for the Operation of Non-Orthodox Religious Communities (Sept. 28, 2009), *available at* http://www.synigoros.gr/?i=human-rights.el.naoi-euktirioi-oikoi.28285 (in Greek).

[432] *Id.*

[433] Kallistos Ware, *Old Calendarists*, *in* MINORITIES IN GREECE, *supra* note 3, at 15.

[434] *Id.*

Orthodox, they fell outside the scope of the 1938 Law. The Council of State resolved this lacuna in 1991, by holding that they are subject to a simpler form of permission.[435]

A number of monks belonging to the Old Calendarists in the Esphigmenou Monastery located in Mount Athos disputed the authority of the Greek Orthodox Patriarchate. In 2003 the Supreme Court of Greece held that the monks should be evicted from the monastery, but the decision was never implemented. The Patriarchate, meanwhile, has officially recognized new monks who deem the presence of the Old Calendarist monks illegal.[436]

In *Vergos v. Greece*,[437] the applicant, a member of the Old Calendarists, applied for permission to build a place of worship on a plot he owned. His request for permission was declined. The Supreme Administrative Court dismissed his appeal on the grounds that the house of worship was a public building and that by law such buildings were not allowed on sites not designated for such use in the urban plan. Building such a place of worship would require a change of the urban plan. The Court also claimed that the applicant was the only member of the Old Calendarists in the region and that there was no social need to alter the plan.

He applied to the ECHR and claimed his freedom of religion was violated by the refusal of the authorities to modify the plan and grant him the needed permission. The ECHR found that the refusal to designate the area for the building of a house of prayer amounted to interference with the applicant's right to the freedom to "manifest his religion through worship and observance." The interference, however, was prescribed by law and pursued a legitimate aim— that is, protection of public order and the rights and freedoms of others. The ECHR noted that the applicant requested an exemption from the preestablished planning regulations and that the Supreme Administrative Court had balanced the individual's right to express and observe his religion against the public interest. Therefore, based on the margin of appreciation granted to contracting states, the ECHR stated that the measure was justified and proportionate to the aim pursued and there was no violation of article 9.

The applicant also argued that the proceedings were excessively long. The Court noted that the proceedings lasted fourteen years, eleven months, and twenty-two days. The Court concluded that such an excessive length of time failed to meet the criterion of "reasonable time" contained in article 6, paragraph 1 of the Convention. Thus, the ECHR unanimously held that there was a violation of article 6.

---

[435] Stavros, *supra* note 40, at 10.

[436] U.S. DEPARTMENT OF STATE, INTERNATIONAL RELIGIOUS FREEDOM REPORT 2010: GREECE (Nov. 17, 2010), http://www.state.gov/j/drl/rls/irf/2010/148940.htm.

[437] Vergos v. Greece, App. No. 924/2004, Eur. Ct. H.R. (June 24, 2004), http://hudoc.echr.coe.int/sites/eng/pages/search.aspx?i=001-61851 (in French).

B. Taking the Oath in Court

The judgment of the ECHR in *Dimitras and Others v. Greece*,[438] issued on June 3, 2010, concerns the obligation of the applicants to indicate their religious convictions when appearing before the court to testify either as witnesses, complainants, or suspects in criminal proceedings. The applicants complained that such a requirement violated the article 9 right to freedom of religion, the article 8 right to respect for privacy and family life, and the article 14 prohibition on discrimination.

The ECHR emphasized its long-held opinion that freedom of thought, conscience, and religion is an essential element of pluralism and constitutes a cornerstone of a democratic society. It also stated that freedom of religion is a critical part of any believer's identity, as well as that of an atheist, agnostic, or skeptic. The ECHR reiterated that freedom to manifest one's religion also included an individual's right not to express a faith or religious conviction. The ECHR noted that the applicants were considered Christian Orthodox as a matter of fact and were required to explain that they were atheists or Jews in order to amend the standard statement to reflect their religious identity.[439]

The government's interference with the applicants' freedom of religion was based on article 218 of the Code of Criminal Procedure governing the taking of the oath on the Bible. The pertinent article was drafted based on the premise that all witnesses were Orthodox Christians and thus would not object to swearing on the Bible as reflected in the already prepared wording of the standard statement. Article 220 of the Code of Criminal Procedure allows exceptions for those who are not Greek Orthodox to take the oath based on their religion, or to make a solemn declaration in the absence of religion or if their religion does not allow them to swear. Moreover, based on article 220, individuals must reveal their religious beliefs if they do not want the presumption of article 218 to apply to them. The ECHR also noted that not only articles 218 and 220 of the Code were incompatible with article 9 of the Convention, but also article 217, which requires all witnesses to state their religion prior to testifying in criminal proceedings. It also noted that the Code of Civil Procedure provided alternatives for witnesses to select when taking a religious oath or making a declaration.[440]

The ECHR found that article 9 was violated by requiring applicants to reveal their religious beliefs in order to be allowed to testify in criminal proceedings and that the government's interference with the right of the applicants not to manifest their religious convictions was neither justified nor proportionate to the aim pursued. The ECHR did not find it necessary to examine whether articles 8 and 14 were also violated.

---

[438] Dimitras and Other v. Greece, App. Nos. 42837/06, 3237/07, 3269/07, 35793/07 and 6099/08, Eur. Ct. H. R. (June 3, 2010), a http://hudoc.echr.coe.int/sites/eng/pages/search.aspx?i=001-99012 (in French). For a non-binding English version of Dimitras and Others v. Greece (No. 2), in which the Court held that the decision was in itself just satisfaction, *see* Press Release of the Registrar of the Court, Judgments Concerning . . . Greece [et al.] (Nov. 3, 2011), http://hudoc.echr.coe.int/sites/eng/pages/search.aspx?i=003-3732289-4257846.

[439] *Id.*

[440] *Id.*

C. Exemption of Minister of Known Religion from Military Service: Georgiadis v. Greece

The case of *Georgiadis v. Greece*[441] involved a Jehovah's Witnesses minister who requested to be exempted from military service pursuant to Law No. 1763/1988, which exempts the ministers of all known religions from military service. The recruitment office rejected his request on the grounds that Jehovah's Witnesses were not a "known" religion. He refused to join his unit and subsequently was found guilty of insubordination. The Athens Permanent Army Tribunal found him not guilty because he was exempted from military service as a minister of a known religion. He was released but still ordered to appear at the appropriate military unit. Subsequently, he was ordered to join the unit on two more occasions. He refused and was charged with insubordination. When he appeared before the Athens Permanent Army Tribunal, and later before the Salonica Permanent Army Tribunal, he was acquitted but with no compensation for his detention pending trial, as provided by law, because his detention was due to "his own gross negligence."[442] Article 533, paragraph 2 of the Code of Criminal Procedure exempts a person from compensation if he or she was detained "intentionally or by gross negligence." The applicant claimed that a civil right to compensation is created when detention follows a conviction that is overturned on appeal.[443]

The applicant complained before the ECHR that he did not receive a fair hearing regarding compensation for his detention. The ECHR observed that article 533, paragraph 2 of the Code of Criminal Procedure creates a right to receive compensation, irrespective of how this right is perceived under domestic law, for an individual who has been unlawfully detained. In examining whether such a right to compensation is a civil right, the ECHR noted that article 6, paragraph 1 of the Convention, pertaining to a right to a fair hearing, applies irrespective of the character of the legislation that governs how the dispute is to be determined. The ECHR noted that for article 533, paragraph 2 to apply, a detention followed by an acquittal must have taken place. The ECHR said these are public law issues, but that the right to compensation created by that provision has a civil character. Consequently, the ECHR concluded that application of article 533 fell within the scope of article 6, paragraph 1 of the Convention. The applicant complained that he did not have an opportunity to be heard regarding his compensation for his detention and that the military courts, *proprio motu*, examined the issue of the state's liability regarding compensation along with his conviction.[444] The ECHR held that the applicant ought to have had the chance to submit to the court his arguments regarding compensation, and that the military courts' decision *proprio motu* on the issue of compensation precluded the applicant from making an application himself. It also found that the army tribunals failed to state reasons for their decision not to grant compensation due to the applicant's "gross negligence" and failed to elaborate on the concept of gross negligence. For all the reasons stated above, the ECHR found Greece in violation of article 6, paragraph 1 of the Convention.[445]

---

[441] Case of Georgiadis v. Greece, App. No. 21522/93, Eur. Ct. H.R. (May 29, 1997), http://hudoc.echr.coe.int/sites/eng/pages/search.aspx?i=001-58037.

[442] *Id.* para. 14.

[443] *Id.* para. 22 (citing Code of Greek Criminal Procedure art. 533).

[444] *Id.* para. 37.

[445] *Id.* paras. 40–43.

D. Legal Personality of Religious Communities

The right to establish religious organizations derives from article 13 of the Greek Constitution, which provides the right to manifest one's religion, and from article 9 in conjunction with article 11 of the of the European Convention on Human Rights. The ECHR has held that the right to religious freedom is not only an individual right but has a collective aspect and must be interpreted and applied in conjunction with article 11 of the Convention, relating to freedom of association, so that religious communities are able to register and exercise their religious beliefs effectively, without government interference.[446] In *Case of the Metropolitan Church of Bessarabia and Others*,[447] which concerned the issues of lack of recognition and lack of a legal personality, the ECHR stated that the applicant church could not operate in the absence of recognition. In particular, its priests could not conduct a divine service, its members could not meet to practice their religion, and, not having legal personality, it was not entitled to judicial protection of its assets.[448] Another issue closely associated with the lack of legal personality of a religious entity is its lack of access to courts, as is clearly illustrated by *Canea Catholic Church v. Greece*, referenced below.

1. Greek Orthodox Church and Jewish Community

In Greece, the Greek Orthodox Church is a legal entity of public law by virtue of article 1(4) of Law No. 590/1977 on the Statutory Charter of the Church of Greece.[449] The Jewish community is also recognized as a legal entity of public law. Law No. 2456/1920 on Jewish Communities granted the right to the Jewish community to establish itself as a legal community in areas where there are more than twenty Jewish families and there is also a synagogue.[450] The same law also granted Jewish communities the right to establish educational institutions and their own curricula as long as such curricula did not impinge on internal legislation and ensured sufficient training of the Greek language. Rabbis are chosen by the Jewish community and appointed after a written endorsement by the Minister of Education and Religious Affairs.[451]

---

[446] See Opinion No. 535/2009 of the European Commission for Democracy Through Law (Venice Commission) on the Legal Status of Religious Communities in Turkey and the Right of the Orthodox Patriarchate of Istanbul to Use the Adjective Ecumenical (Mar. 2010), http://www.venice.coe.int/docs/2010/CDL-AD(2010)005-f.pdf (in French). *See also* Lance S. Lehnhof, *Freedom of Religious Association: The Right of Religious Organizations to Obtain Legal Entity Status Under the European Convention*, 2002 BYU L. Rev. 561.

[447] *Id.*

[448] Case of Metropolitan Church of Bessarabia and Others v. Moldova, para. 129, App. No. 45701/99, Eur. Ct. H.R. (2001), *cited in id.*, http://hudoc.echr.coe.int/sites/eng/pages/search.aspx?i=001-59985.

[449] E.K.E.D., Part A, No. 146 (1977), http://www.et.gr/index.php?option=com_wrapper&view=wrapper&Itemid=108&lang=el (click on number and year).

[450] Law 2456/1920 on Jewish Communities art. 1, E.K.E.D., Part A., No. 173, *available at* http://www.et.gr/idocs-nph/search/pdfViewerForm html?args=5C7QrtC22wFDzYxnlR7N6ndtvSoClr L8LHF9k8yiZ3t5MXD0LzQTLWPU9yLzB8V68knBzLCmTXKaO6fpVZ6Lx3UnKl3nP8NxdnJ5r9cmWyJWelDv WS_18kAEhATUkJb0x1LIdQ163nV9K--td6SIuR1E0vVH8pamIrZh-nxNikSpOWYZgn4ow-6OiBI8XpLH.

[451] *Id.* art. 5.

2. Muslim Community

The legal personality of the Muslim community in general, which is distinct from those who belong to the Muslim minority and live in Thrace, was recognized as early as 1913 by article 13 of Protocol No. 3 to the Treaty of Peace between Greece and Turkey concluded in Athens.[452] Article 11 of the Treaty of Athens, granted a number of rights to Muslims, including equality before the law, and the right to religious freedom and religious autonomy.

On the other hand, the newly settled Muslims who are of various ethnic origin and other immigrants who moved to Greece following migratory flows from Asia, Africa, and the Middle East in the early 1990s are not considered minorities by Greece. This is in line with the policy of most European states, which do not view immigrants as minorities. A number of authors refer to the recently settled Muslims in Greece as "New Islam" to distinguish them from those living in Thrace who compose the "Old Islam."[453] Most of the late-settled Muslims live around the Athens region.

While there are close to 300 mosques in Western Thrace and a few on the islands of Rhodes and Cos, there is still no mosque in Athens to serve the religious needs of the Muslims. The first place used for prayers by Muslims was operated in 1990 on top of a hotel; currently there are a great number of such places in garages, basements, and other locations. Pakistanis have seven prayer halls, Bangladeshis five, and Egyptians three.[454] The requests for building mosques is an issue that has sparked controversy among citizens, the Greek Church, and the Greek government.

Law No. 3512/2006 on a Mosque in Athens authorizes the construction of a mosque on public land that will be provided by the Greek State.[455] Pursuant to Law 3512/2006 the mosque will be built in the greater Athens area to enable Muslims who live in Athens to exercise their religious rights. Construction expenses will be covered by the Program of Public Expenditures. Law No. 3512/2006 also provides for the creation of a nonprofit legal entity called the Managing Council of the Athenian Mosque. The Council will have its seat in the Athens area and will be under the supervision of the Minister of Education and Religion. Its main task will be the management and maintenance of the mosque. The public land was designated in 2011 by Law No. 4014/2011 dealing with environmental permits and illegally constructed houses.[456] The Law explicitly states that a piece of land of 850 square meters in the Botanicos area is granted by the State for the building of a mosque along with other facilities, as needed to assist the operation of

---

[452] Konstantinos Tsitselikis, *The Legal Status of Islam in Greece*, *in* 44(3) DIE WELT DES ISLAMS 404 (2004).

[453] Angeliki Ziaka, *Muslims and Muslim Education in Greece*, *in* EDNAN ASLAN, ISLAMIC EDUCATION IN EUROPE 141 (2009). *See also* Tsitselikis, *supra* note 452, at 406–07.

[454] Ziaka, *supra* note 453, at 157–59.

[455] E.K.E.D., Part. A, No. 264 (2006), *available at* http://www.et.gr/index.php?option=com_wrapper& view=wrapper&Itemid=104&lang=el.

[456] E.K.E.D., Part A, No. 209 (2011), *available at* http://www.et.gr/index.php?option=com_wrapper& view=wrapper&Itemid=104&lang=el.

the mosque. Ownership of the mosque will belong to the Greek State.[457] An imam will be appointed, for a two-year renewable term. The imam will be paid by the Ministry of Religion and Education.

To meet the demands of a growing number of Muslim immigrants, Protestants, and others, a 2006 decree allowed the cremation of foreigners or Greeks who wish to be cremated in line with their religious beliefs.[458] The Orthodox Church, which staunchly opposed the decree's application to the Greek Orthodox population, has accepted that priests will perform funeral services as long as they are not informed of the cremation. The first crematorium was expected to be in operation at the end of 2011.[459]

3. Roman Catholic Church

The legal status of the Roman Catholic Church in Greece is complex and ambiguous. The Supreme Court has dealt with two key issues: (a) whether Greek Roman Catholics are allowed to apply canon law as far as their personal status;[460] and (b) whether the Roman Catholic Church and its bishoprics, monasteries, and foundations have legal personality. Those bishoprics, monasteries, and foundations that were established prior to the establishment of the Greek State in 1830 are recognized as legal entities, without having to fulfill any legal requirements. The Supreme Court has affirmed their legal status in numerous decisions, one of which is discussed below.[461]

In 1994, the Supreme Court in Decision No. 360/1994 reversed its 150-year-old firm position and held that Catholic monasteries and churches that have not acquired legal personality pursuant to the Civil Code provisions are not legal entities and therefore lack legal standing before the courts. It emphasized that having legal personality is a prerequisite for a house of prayer to be able to represent itself before the courts.[462] This decision was challenged before the ECHR in the case of *Canea Catholic Church v. Greece*.[463]

The case first arose in the district court of Canea in Crete when the Roman Catholic Church filed a legal action against its neighbors/defendants who had demolished part of its surrounding wall. The defendants raised the issue of lack of legal personality of the Roman Catholic Church and argued it therefore lacked *locus standi* before the court. The Court of Peace agreed with the plaintiff Church. On appeal, the court of first instance in Canea quashed the decision of the Court of Peace and stated that the Treaty of Sèvres guarantees freedom of religion

---

[457] *Id.*

[458] Law 3448/2006 art. 35, E.K.E.D., Part A, No. 57, *available at* http://www.et.gr/index.php?option=com_wrapper&view=wrapper&Itemid=108&lang=el.

[459] Damian Mac Con Uladh, *First Greek Crematorium On the Way*, ATHENS NEWS (Dec. 5, 2010), http://www.athensnews.gr/issue/13420/34712.

[460] ANDROUTSOPOULOS, *supra* note 405, at 119.

[461] *Id.* at 128.

[462] *Id.* at 130.

[463] Case of the Canea Catholic Church v. Greece, *supra* note 108.

and worship to all, irrespective of religious denomination. However, the court noted, for any religious denomination to acquire legal personality, it must comply with certain legal requirements. The court found that the Church had not done so and that canon law that regulates the status of the Church had not been adopted.

The Catholic Church, in instituting a complaint before the ECHR, claimed that denial of the Church's legal personality amounted to discriminatory interference with its right of access to the courts, freedom of religion, and peaceful enjoyment of its possessions. Greece argued that the applicant Church had not *ipso facto* acquired a legal personality due to a lack of compliance with domestic legislation. The ECHR rejected Greece's argument and held that such a formality restricted the Church's "right to a court" and therefore constituted a violation of article 6 of the European Convention of Human Rights. The Court, upon noting that no such restrictions are imposed on the Orthodox Church or the Jewish community, which have unfettered power to take legal action and protect their property rights in court with no extra formality, held that article 14 of the European Convention was violated, since "no objective and reasonable justification for such difference in treatment" existed. The ECHR also observed that it was not concerned with whether the Catholic Church was a legal entity of public or private law, since this was a matter of domestic law.[464]

In compliance with the above decision of the ECHR, Greece enacted Law No. 2731/1999,[465] which added to those legal entities that were kept in force based on article 13 of the Introductory Law of the 1946 Greek Civil Code the legal entities established or operating prior to 1946 that belonged to the Catholic Church.[466] Article 13 of the Introductory Law simply maintained in force those legal entities that were legally established at the time of the entry into force of the Civil Code.[467] It remains unclear as to the status of those legal entities established after 1946, because this provision neither clarifies nor provides for their fate.[468]

4. Other Religious Communities

Other religious groups have the right to be established as legal entities pursuant to the pertinent provisions of the Greek Civil Code, either as associations (art. 78 *et seq.*), as foundations that are approved by a decree (art. 108 *et seq.*), or as charitable fund-raising committees (art. 122 *et seq.*). Registration of associations is governed by articles 78–81 of the Civil Code and article 107 of its Introductory Law.[469] An application and the bylaws of the association must be filed with the appropriate court. An association must fulfill four

---

[464] Under Greek law, a legal entity can be either of a public or private nature or of a mixed character. A legal entity of public law is established by the state for a public, governmental, or quasi-governmental purpose and is governed by public law, whereas a legal entity of private law is one whose purpose is private, for profit or nonprofit, and is governed by private law. Symeon Symeonidis, *The General Principles of Civil Law, in* INTRODUCTION TO GREEK LAW 84 (Konstantinos D. Kerameus & Phaedon J. Kozyris eds., 2008).

[465] Law 2731/1999, E.K.E.D., Part A, No. 138 (1999).

[466] *Id.* art. 33.

[467] Introductory Law to the Civil Code art. 13, *in* SPYRIDAKIS, *supra* note 153, at 565.

[468] ANDROUTSOPOULOS, *supra* note 405, at 141.

[469] General Principles of the Civil Code arts. 78–81, 108, *in* SPYRIDAKIS, *supra* note 153, at 32, 33, 41.

requirements: the religious group must belong to a known religion, the bylaws must be signed by at least twenty persons, the association must be of a nonprofit nature, and its purpose must not negatively affect public order or morals.

VII. Conclusion

Since the Lausanne Treaty was concluded in 1923, international law on minorities has evolved noticeably from the principle of nondiscrimination to requiring positive measures by states to promote and protect distinct rights of minorities related to their own language, religion, and culture. In the meantime, Greece has gained a deeper understanding of the issues involved, as reflected in its new policy adopted in the early 1990s urging equality in law and equal citizenship for its Muslim minority.

There are indications that Greece is retreating from the reciprocity principle, as reflected in the law on *vakfs*, which denounces reciprocity, and the law on taxation of *vakfs*, which makes no reference to it. Overall, and in conformity with the Treaty of Lausanne, Greece has fulfilled its basic obligations toward its Muslim minority in Western Thrace. The right to association of those Muslims who seek to register as Turkish rather than Muslims is curtailed and the ECHR has found that Greece is in breach of article 11 of the right of association of the ECHRFF. At the same time, Greece's efforts to comply and expedite execution of judgments issued by the ECHR in general is indicative of a trend toward abandoning controlling practices against freedom of religion in favor of pluralism and acceptance of all individuals in its territory.

For those who self-identify as Slavo-Macedonians, the most pressing issue is related to the denial of the right of association under the name "Macedonian," in conformity with the ECHR decisions. This is an extremely challenging issue for Greece for which there is no easy solution due to the complexity and inherent political undertones of the issue.

For the Roma, the areas of housing and education are still problematic, as amply illustrated by the case law referenced in the pertinent section on Roma. It is axiomatic that legislation and policy programs by themselves will not affect change, unless the existing legal framework is implemented effectively and social attitudes toward Roma are also altered.

By enacting Law No. 3305/2005 in implementation of the EU directives, Greece has taken steps to fight discrimination in general based on race, ethnic origin, religion, or belief in the areas of employment, occupation, social protection, and services. Another positive measure in fighting racism based on religion is the February 2011 draft bill, which criminalizes incitement and the commission of acts likely to lead to violence or hatred against persons or groups on the basis of their religion.

Prepared by Theresa Papademetriou
Senior Foreign Law Specialist
October 2012